FREAK MAGNET

Everyone does have a back story

By
LAURA SPENDLOVE CRAPO

ISBN

Paperback: 979-8-90321-078-7

Hardback: 979-8-90321-079-4

Dedication

This book is dedicated to our beloved Uncle Frank Bennion.

Table of Contents

The truth is out.

I'm Rachel Petty, and I can't say my judgment of character has always been spot-on. This was confirmed at my 20th birthday party. My loving sisters, Suzanne, Jennifer, and Jane, played the old Rick James' hit "Super Freak" while presenting me with their gift. It was a big navy blue T-shirt with "FREAK MAGNET" emblazoned on the front.

This spurred lots of laughter from the family and me. It was embarrassing for me, but I not only knew it was true—I lived it. So, there's some explaining to do. My weird dates and acquaintances have inspired this to happen.

There is a combination in my mindset that's the catalyst here. The mixture of me being nice, wanting to be liked, being curious, and, ashamedly gullible was the trigger.

This has never been a serious ranking. There have been times when I've simply been attracted to these guys. Me, being a Freak Magnet has always been more humorous than anything. I've always respected the opinion of my family and would keep that in mind. My Freak Magnet has always been a mere thumbs up or thumbs down, a hit or miss. And, on the bright side, these experiences are something I can laugh about.

Backing way up

I was extremely shy as a kid. I liked playing, reading, and being with my family. I thought I was normal. Then there was one time at a church social when a few women passing by noticed me and said, "Hmm, I didn't know the Pettys had another daughter."

What?! Was I invisible? That was the first time I noticed how people saw—or didn't see—me. Then the review went on.

I enjoyed school and made friends with the other kids. There were white, Black, and lots of Mexican students at the school. I accepted the mixture of people without any issues.

In elementary school, my friend Laura Ortiz asked if we could walk to school together. Her house was on my way to school, so I would stop by. A few times, I got there before she was done with her breakfast. She used a tortilla to wipe her plate as she finished eating. Hmm, that was different, but understandable because our families were different. We always had toasted bread with butter in the morning.

In the fifth grade, my teacher, Mrs. Rodich, told me her grandfather had carved the seagull used on Temple Square's arched entry in Salt Lake City, Utah. I told her, "Oh, that's great!" I had never mentioned that I was a member of The Church of Jesus Christ of Latter-day Saints. So that was interesting. But I was the sixth of the Petty family's seven kids attending the school, and the teachers took notice apparently.

A new epiphany was learning more about the Catholic faith. I was confused by the smudges on my classmates' foreheads and asked my friend Ruthie Moran about it. She simply said that it was for Ash Wednesday. I soon learned it had to do with the week before Easter.

Later that school year, my friend Katie Rojas told me her

brother Frankie had broken his femur. I said, "That's sad—how did it happen?" She filled me in on the details and told me they were praying to Saint Judas for help. I had no idea praying to saints was a thing and chuckled.

Katie was unhappy with my response. She told me Saint Judas was the "saint of lost causes." I explained that I didn't know that and apologized. I had a lot to learn and, in that case, I was the freak.

Another young experience was having my friend Anna Beck from down the street tell me her dad liked me the best. I was surprised and asked her why. He liked me best from our group of friends because I didn't swear.

That was another interesting thing to notice. I never knew how that conversation came up between them. In my family, we didn't swear, so I didn't either. My parents, Bill and Brenda Petty, are good people. They weren't preachy but simply set an example and taught us about Jesus Christ and His gospel. I knew what their expectations were.

Then racial integration started coming into play. The Los Angeles Unified School District decided they would help us make friends between races. We students were bewildered by this goal. We had a field trip to the Watts Towers in a sketchy L.A. neighborhood. The local students in that area were mostly African-American. My school had some African-Americans, but the other students were Mexican or white.

It was mostly an awkward trip. The towers were very interesting, and we did say "hi" to each other. Walter was the only other student I talked to long enough to ask his name. So, there was bemusement, but no new enlightenment for sudden world peace.

More differences coming my way

My first day at San Fernando Junior High School started with a big Chola blocking my way. A Chola (feminine) or a Cholo (masculine) is a tough Hispanic. My new "friend" asked, "Where do you think you're going?" I was scared.

She was literally a foot taller than me, and she wasn't smiling. I told her I was just looking for my first class. When she saw me clutching my class schedule in my sweaty little hands, she let me pass. Phew! I wouldn't have even known where to start fighting someone that big. And a skinny little white girl wasn't worth her time.

The new kicker for this racial integration was decided: we were told half of my eighth-grade class—myself included—was being bused to another school.

For the first part of the year, we were bused to Lawrence Jr. High in Chatsworth, CA. The other half of the students were bused in the second half of the year.

They were mostly white, upper-class kids, and I asked my teacher if I had to go. "I'm white," I said. But she said, "Yes, you have to go." So I had no wiggle room there.

That was a harsh lesson—being forced into two very different student bodies. They were mostly accepting at first. And I did get to meet Debbie, who ate lox with cream cheese on a bagel for lunch every day. That was a unique detail to learn about her and the Jewish culture. She was very nice, so I was pleased with that new friendship.

Things went south as the semester proceeded. I had signed up to be an office aide while at Lawrence Jr. High. The women in the office were very nice until realizing I was one of "them."

They mentioned a last name, Rikule, and I said I had neighbors on my street with that last name. They asked where I lived, and their demeanor quickly shifted when I told them. That was another difference I observed. I was disappointed in their behavior, and I didn't like it.

It was even more difficult to watch as the school year wrapped up. The San Fernando Jr. High students were tired of being looked down on and treated poorly. They were mainly Hispanics—and my friends!

So, I watched from a distance as the fighting broke out. The San Fernando students took out their vengeance on the Lawrence students. It was understandable when looking at it with empathy, but it was a difficult thing to witness as well.

As my life progressed, my 'freak magnet' prowess became more questionable. Its accuracy was shaky because I was still quite young and experiencing different things for the first time. My life flight was encountering some turbulence. And, high school was going to be another new and challenging venture. However, I had some toughness and would not crumble.

Go Spartans!

I enjoyed attending Sylmar High. My fellow students were nice. There were the Stoners, the Surfers, and the Jocks. Rumor held that a narcotics officer was there posing as a student because of the heavy drug use. I knew who I could ask for the "best snow" (AKA cocaine) or marijuana.

It was somehow touching to have my cheerleading friends make sure there was Sprite to drink at our practices. "Rachel can't drink Coke," they would say. I never told them that, nor had I shared that I was a member of The Church of Jesus Christ of Latter-day Saints, a "Mormon," but somehow word spreads. I was using the word "interesting" more and more as I reviewed my interactions.

A new revelation of opinion came to my notice through my friend Darrell, who told me I should wear silver jewelry, not gold. He was a big African-American football player on our school's team. Darrell explained that gold jewelry looked better on dark skin and silver jewelry on light skin. His girlfriend, Roberta, practiced with our cheer squad and was better than most of us. It was sobering to learn that she couldn't join us because her family couldn't afford cheer camp or the uniforms. I was learning how oblivious I could be to others and their situations.

Then there was the faculty. Some teachers at Sylmar High were antagonistic when I was in their class. I was the sixth of the school's seven Petty children they had taught, so they knew I was one of those peculiar "Mormons." Plus, between my mom and dad, different intensities of red hair ran in the family. Truthfully, I was grateful to have a beautiful auburn shade—nothing too attention-grabbing. But we were easy to spot, apparently.

Ms. Paul, my English teacher, knew where I came from and dissuaded me from taking the difficult AP English exam. She said I probably wouldn't pass it. However, she loved Lois, who was also in the class. Lois should definitely take the AP English exam, which clearly showed me where I stood with her. Well, I did take it—and passed! Passing that AP exam gave me four credits toward my college courses!

That was my way of quietly and smugly sticking my tongue out at Ms. Paul. To be honest, beyond her dislike of me, Ms. Paul's credibility was shot when she told us the best moisturizer was Crisco and that we should spread it all over our dry skin. Some teachers don't give their students any credit for having perceptive abilities (i.e., she thought we were stupid).

The antagonism became a little more direct. My history teacher, Mr. Talbot, was "teaching" about the building up of the West in the United States. He scoffed about Brigham Young taking charge of the pioneers—"those believers." He made light of the canal, irrigation, and street organization he had put into place. What a weak educator, downplaying the importance of transportation, irrigation, and harvesting to a new society!

Then, there was Mr. Johnson, the biology teacher. He spoke directly about his dislike for Brigham Young University. What kind of college tells students how to behave, what they can wear, or how long the men's hair should be? He would openly demean BYU's merit. I had a distinct awareness of where these teachers were aiming their criticism.

Then again, this was a teacher who didn't really read the one-page weekly homework we submitted. Mr. Johnson would just put a quick check mark at the top of the page. I gave my theory a try by starting with solid facts per the topic being studied. Then it was just gibberish and nonsense. "The ankle bone's connected to the knee bone; the knee bone's connected to the hip bone. If you're a pepper, I'm a pepper. Blah blah blah." Then I wrote a serious ending paragraph. He never caught on to what I was doing.

One teacher who was supportive of positive behavior regardless of your persuasion was Mr. Muncy. He was my English teacher in 11th grade. I loved the point he made one day that swearing was a sign of weak vocabulary. He said cussing was lazy and like watching black-and-white TV, while using deeper, thoughtful, more creative words was a more intelligent way to speak in technicolor.

In that same class, he asked us to break into groups and read *Walter Mitty* aloud. I determined to read it like it was written—swear words and all. It wasn't comfortable. The sweet protection from my classmates came out. They told me, "Rachel, you don't have to say everything." Again, I'd never spelled out my beliefs, but it echoed my elementary school friend's dad's compliment. People **do** notice things.

Mr. Anspacher, my Government teacher, was my saving grace at Sylmar High. He was super intelligent and very kind—the sort of person you knew could have a more elevated position elsewhere. But I was very thankful to have him as my teacher. One day, he asked the class to give him one word to describe ourselves. As he went around the room, I didn't want to say anything stupid or too cocky. I chose "Capable," and he repeated it and said, "Very good," with a nod. I don't think he knew how gratifying that was.

Fortunately, my fellow students didn't treat me rudely or any differently. Except one day, John John said something I didn't like. He was Black, a cool friend, and a yell leader in our cheer squad. We were practicing and chatting when he said, "You sound like you're from Utah or something." I rejected that opinion because I was a cool, born-and-raised Californian! Didn't he know that?!

The last stark difference I noticed in high school was when my friend Julie clapped and cheered when the radio club announced over the loudspeaker that a local politician had been shot and injured. I was appalled! Who likes it when other people are hurt? I started seeing my naiveté in the world.

Lessons learned

My new acquaintances and dates which eventually triggered the gift of my FREAK MAGNET t-shirt were a potpourri of confusion and poor choices. I had one date that ended up at a creepy and crowded arcade. It was a bad-smelling last choice. (Obviously, his budget was tight.) He started mentioning a new lightweight plastic engine for motorcycles.

Wow, I didn't put 2+2 together on that one. Duh—of course a plastic combustion engine would melt. This guy was just throwing that out to see how long it would take me to catch on.

I've always tended to leave all possibilities open for the hmm, 'what-ifs?' But, I'm not stupid. So I cleverly maneuvered around some difficult situations.

My 'give it a try' approach was the trap door to my social life. But, I learned that no situation or person was a guaranteed good choice. And luckily no option I chose was dangerous, a real risk, or anything that took too much of my time.

On the bright side, these "friendships" were very short-lived. For example, the arcade guy telling me about the plastic engine was as shallow as a little Arizona puddle on a hot day.

His name was Marco Dubois, and he was very handsome with curly black hair and brown eyes. He was very aware that he was the "cool guy" with a cool name. We were playing a video game at the arcade when he started kissing my neck and hugging me! No chit-chat, no looking me in the eye?! No gracias; no melting at the knees for me. Sayonara, Marco!

Another dead-end conversation happened at a community Valentine's Day dance. This guy, Gus, with his nicely combed light brown hair and blue eyes, tried coaching me about the highlights of Scientology. He used Tom Cruise as an example of being successful through their teachings.

"There's no limit to the success a person can have, and the teachings of Scientology are helping people be their best." My goodness, I was half expecting him to break into a cheer and teach me their motto!

I'm honest and nice, but I hadn't signed up for a self-help coaching session. He is the only person to whom I've intentionally given a wrong phone number.

Mike was another dance discovery. He was a cute and cool guy with a great blond flat-top. I had fun talking to him, and I gave him my correct phone number. So he asked me out and came to our house to pick me up.

He had a short-sleeve, muscle-displaying T-shirt on with a big bulldog tattoo on his big upper arm. I was surprised, but church dances didn't require long-sleeve shirts, so I wasn't aware he had that. Still, I thought it wasn't a big deal.

Well, we went to dinner, and a conversation started. I saw a red flag when his first question was, "What's the worst thing you've ever done?" My mind was scrambling, and the worst thing I came up with was playing pranks at girls' camp. Oh my, what a villain I was—ha-ha.

Then he said he seriously injured a guy during a bar fight when he kicked his opponent hard in the ribs. It was another no-thanks moment. There was no substance there, and we obviously didn't have anything in common. So that was another first and last date.

But wait, there's more! There was a crash-and-burn relationship with Ross. He was nice enough and handsome, with perfectly combed dark brown hair. But he was creepy in an "I know better than you" kind of way.

I thought it was over until I realized he had followed me home from work one evening and left a note on my car. It said that I was like a ripe peach, and he was interested in making a relationship with me. Say what?!

There's more—he was at church and again followed me out after the meetings were over. He told me he was a returned missionary and had had a spiritual experience telling him we should be together. Yikes!

Yes, I'm nice, but I clearly let him know that I was not interested. He wasn't the only one the Spirit speaks to, and I never received that message. Yay, me!!

Double dates are double trouble

I'm a good friend, almost too good. My double dates have been my worst dates. When my friend Lisa asked me to go on a double date with her and her boyfriend and his friend, I was skeptical (starting to catch on, right?). She assured me he was a really nice guy and it would be fun—not so.

We went to Baskin-Robbins for ice cream to begin with. Bob, my date, wore a high-buttoned polo shirt and a tightly belted pair of khakis. Hmm, he was quite a clothes horse, but not very handsome.

He made sure everyone knew bubble-gum ice cream was his favorite. That's fine—to each his own. But he couldn't take his eyes off Lisa. She's pretty, blonde, and bubbly, but it was almost comical how he was ignoring me.

The "fun" date continued when we went dancing. I love dancing, and it was fun. Then, amidst the dance moves, Bob dropped his cell phone. We all searched between the feet and the side tables until we found it. It was a very interesting, unfun date—the kind of date you can laugh at five years later.

Bob was understandably infatuated with Lisa, which was fine by me. I helped complete the quartet—end of story.

The second double date occurred when Amanda begged me to go on a double date. Her boyfriend, Sam, was from the Mideast and had a friend, Job, who had just been dumped. They had already purchased tickets for the Air Supply Reunion concert at the Hollywood Bowl. I finally caved and went with them.

What happened next was surprising and a real head-shaker. After getting seated, I tried to make small talk with my sullen date. I asked him where he was from, and he abruptly said, "Jordan." That was the beginning and end of our conversation.

When the concert began, the stage started unfolding with multi-colored lights and billowing fog. My date and Sam stood up and were shouting, "Allah! It's like Allah is coming!" I was bemused and somewhat embarrassed. However, they sang every word of the songs being played. Wow—they were genuine fans, which surprised me!

During the concert, Job left to get a treat without a word. He came back with white wine and peanuts and enjoyed them until the concert was over. The parking lot was packed, and just as we got to the car, Job threw up everything we thought was possible.

We got in while Sam sprayed Polo cologne to improve the smell—which was unsuccessful. They had made dinner reservations at the fancy Bonaventure Hotel with its silver cylindrical towers in Los Angeles. We left Job in the car when we got there.

The three of us enjoyed a nice dinner, and Sam let us know that Job had smoked a joint before the concert. Apparently, white wine, peanuts, and marijuana don't mix.

This was confirmed when we saw puddles of vomit covered with napkins on the parking garage floor around Sam's car. Saying it was an awkward drive home with the lingering odors was an understatement.

I learned some new things that night and never took Amanda's bait again.

Moving on to higher education

Attending Brigham Young University in Provo, Utah, was refreshing. I wasn't one of the handful of "Mormons" in the school. It was enjoyable to share beliefs with the other students and to have professors teaching things in accordance with the Gospel of Jesus Christ. It was strengthening and a relief. We had opening prayers in class, in devotionals, and even at football games—which was new!

It wasn't all religion, all the time. For goodness' sake, the logistics alone were a big change. I went from San Fernando, California, at 600 feet above sea level to Provo's almost 4,500 feet above sea level. I seriously got dizzy or a little faint at first, but after a few weeks, I was accustomed to the change in altitude.

The difference in temperature was almost the deal-breaker. The first time it got so cold my nose froze together, I was ready to reserve a flight back home. Luckily, my frozen nostrils only lasted a few moments and stopped any travel plans.

However, I was the freak when my first response to falling snow was to get out my umbrella. One of my roommates was also from California, and we thought it was the practical thing to do. When something's falling down, that's what you do, right? Oh no, when I saw the smiles and head shakes, it was apparently not the way to handle snow and cold temperatures. So, I conformed to fit in and stay warm with beanies, gloves, and hooded coats.

There was one sneaky threat that was another painful novelty to me: black ice! It takes your feet out so quickly that you don't have any time to brace yourself. Plus, my first encounter with black ice was when I was wearing high heels with my Sunday dress. And I broke a nail!

It was another lesson needing to be learned, dang it! I started watching for patches of concrete or asphalt that looked shiny or wet.

I walked with someone whose arm I could grab if I slipped, and I started wearing safer shoes.

One winter event was unfortunately comical to me—but not to the young woman on crutches who fell down into a perfect X. Her arms and legs were spread out with her face down. I was too far away to help, but that visual makes me chuckle to this day. She was wearing a thick parka and snow boots, so she thankfully wasn't hurt, and others rushed in to help her.

Roll call!

After the excitement of being accepted to BYU, I had to take care of the basics. I chose student housing in Heritage Halls with five unknown roommates. That's another story all to itself.

Then I checked the location and the all-important list of class schedules. I was taking twelve credits and started with general education classes and a mandatory religion class. For that class, I took Book of Mormon 101. My major was undetermined, but I was interested in interior design and art history. I could design good-looking outfits and rooms. I also loved the idea of art conservation and repairing old paintings.

It was so enjoyable and interesting to meet so many new people and learn so many new things! Being exposed to a great variety of new concepts and personalities was satisfying. Cooking for myself started with Top Ramen and homemade banana bread because they were cheap. Wow, I never gave my mom enough credit for all she cooked and did to run our home. Moving up to grilled cheese sandwiches and tomato soup was my new comfort food.

The men were not freakish at all, which was all right. Going to Church on Sundays and weekend dances were something of a meat market. It was an underlying understanding. We young women were checking out the young men and making mental scoring notes. I went on a few dates without sparks. But there were so many group activities that the socialization was built into the school year.

One activity I loved, but that turned out to be terrifying, was my first BYU football game. It's a great stadium with a huge seating capacity and beautiful mountains as a backdrop. However, the foot-stomping to amplify school spirit sounded like an earthquake to me. Having experienced the real thing, I knew what could happen after that sound started.

I was shouting for everybody to stop. Luckily, no one heard me, and I privately calmed down. Phew! Who wants to be labeled the freak? It reminded me of grabbing the center wheel on Disney's teacups ride because I wanted my siblings to stop the spinning.

My classes went well, but interior design wasn't for me. When I thought my layouts and designs were great, the professor had a different opinion. I realized I wasn't as thick-skinned as I thought. But that's what your freshman year is all about, right?

I researched art conservation training. But it seemed very difficult to be accepted. Women applicants were very limited and generally refused. Reading between the lines, they wanted to avoid losing female candidates due to marriage and pregnancy.

Schools teaching art conservation were located in New York, USA, and Italy. So I stuck with Art History, which I loved. I planned on searching out small, privately funded conservation training courses someday.

Home sweet home

After getting home after my first year at BYU, I got a job at Toyota Central in downtown Los Angeles. My friend Todd, who got me the job, was driving—thank goodness.

It was an office job and another opportunity to meet new people and learn new things. Making the office's coffee was one of my assigned tasks. This was both ironic and funny.

I don't drink coffee, but I noticed most people added the cream powder to their cup of Joe. So, I thought it would be a good idea to add the cream to the coffee in the coffee maker. Two birds with one stone, right? Well, I didn't realize that would make the coffee light brown. It was a very obvious mistake, so I threw it away and made more. I was glad that taking out the garbage wasn't my job.

The people in the office were nice and fun to meet. However, one day, one of the salesmen came in for coffee. (It was just coffee.) We chatted a little bit, and he told me there was something different about me. Then he asked me what made me different.

It was his question—what had he noticed? He was about fifteen years older than me, and I hoped he wasn't flirting. So I finally said something my dad would say: "It must be that good clean living," I said with a smile and a chin twitch to the left.

He just smiled back and said, "Maybe that's it." He shrugged his shoulders and went back to work. It wasn't a smooth reply and left me wondering who the freak was here. That question stuck in my mind after that conversation.

The only bummer about that job was the homemade Philippine spring rolls Floyd brought to share. Anyone who has had food poisoning can understand that profound nausea. My sweet Mom drove all the way down to central L.A. with a bucket and towel to pick me up.

Beyond the new experiences I gained in that job, the summer was fun at home spending time with my family. My sisters and I went to some movies and shopped. It was a good break, and I was ready to drive back to BYU.

My paradigm in thinking was beginning to shift. Obviously, I was becoming more adult-ish, and I felt prompted to settle into my beliefs and goals. This was in the back of my mind as I registered for my second year at BYU. I decided to make this a productive year.

Go Cougars!!!

For my second year, I decided to live in an off-campus apartment with roommates who were a mix of friends and strangers. It was a fun year, and we enjoyed each other's company.

My classes were mostly a success. I registered for an Old Testament class because it fit into my schedule. The first day in that class was a revelation that I was an uninformed Bible freak.

I sat down and was comfortable—until I looked at the chalkboard. The penmanship was alright, but I didn't understand a thing! You'd think a college professor would present things more clearly. My judgment was clamped down when I realized he was writing in Hebrew! My bad. Apparently, I had missed the notice that a prerequisite class was required.

Wow, that put me in my place, but in a good way. I made a schedule change to a more understandable religion class, which was New Testament in English. It made me want to learn more about the scriptures. The Bible and the Book of Mormon had always been in my home and discussed at church. I was inspired to have a better understanding of Jesus Christ's gospel and the religion in which I was raised and baptized. I needed to dig deeper into my study and worship.

The science class I registered for was Geography, and again I discovered I had much to learn. Of course, I could point out the continents around the world, but I'd never really zoomed in. Studying the borders, mountain ranges, climate, and culture was fascinating. But it made me aware of how much I didn't know about people's customs around the world, and I was curious.

That second year, I worked part-time in the Administration Building, which was an easy front-desk secretary job. For my P.E. requirement, I signed up for racquetball, which I love. I also enjoyed my Creative Writing class, which counted toward a Communications degree. And the good friends I made, along with the BYU football games, completed an enjoyable year.

The only guy I liked that last semester was Jack, who was no freak. He liked me more than I liked him. He was very nice, but was not for me. During a movie night in a friend's apartment, we sat on the floor to watch. Jack rubbed the back of my neck with his thumb in so many circles it almost hurt. That wasn't the deal-breaker, but I did break up with him soon after. I was nice and told him he could do better elsewhere because he was a great guy. I really did mean it.

Of course, I wanted to find a good man and get married. Those were dreams and goals I had had for years, and my hope remained strong. However, my practical reasoning said, Well, no one has asked me, so…? I held on and kept my eyes open and head on a swivel. What a strategic game romance can be, I chuckled to myself.

Back home for the summer

This was a pivotal time for me. I had been brewing on all those things I had realized I didn't know. Praying more sincerely for guidance and direction was a new commitment. After becoming aware of so many unknowns in my capacity and my future, I started rethinking several things.

Jesus Christ was becoming more real to me, and asking Him for advice was natural. I also had a good time talking with my parents about what I was thinking. I love them both dearly, and I know they love me. They were supportive in my questioning and had solid suggestions.

Having an obnoxious interaction at my summer job with a coworker at Robinson's was ironic. Here I had been contemplating things religious when my summer job in the classy department store provided an interesting wake-up call.

This woman in the makeup and fragrance department (where I didn't work) stopped me as I was walking through. She said, "Are you a Mormon?" I was surprised at this unexpected question, but answered, "Yes, I am." Her rude retort was, "I'm surprised because most of you have that mouse-y brown hair!"

I just shook my head and said, "Dang! What kind of person insults complete strangers?" I walked on, knowing I had to rethink my freak-or-no-freak judgment litmus test. There are millions of types of people a person can meet. And, apparently, it can't be a simple black-and-white call (and that's not skin color).

After that sour interaction, the store manager came walking my way. He said, "Hi, Rebecca – how are you?!" I responded, "It's Rachel, and I'm doing pretty well, thanks."

Then, an unexpected question came to mind. I blurted out, "Hey, Mr. Rasmussen, I was planning to work here just for the summer before going back to BYU. But could I keep working here?" I was surprised when he motioned for me to follow him.

We walked into his office, and he asked his secretary to bring him my file (after I confirmed my name). He flipped my folder open and began reading aloud, "Hmm, 777 North Workman St. – you must have a lucky house." I nodded in agreement, having no idea what he was talking about. He continued by saying that if I moved, I would be SOL, and again, I was clueless as to what that stood for, but gathered that being S.O.L. was not a good thing. I smiled and said, "Yep!"

He had a quizzical expression, and it was like I could read his mind: *What an airhead!* Mr. Rasmussen glanced at my file again and nodded. Seeing my punctuality, great customer service, and no misbehavior marks, he smiled. "Rachel!" he emphasized my name correctly and said he would be privileged to have me stay on as long as I'd like.

Full disclosure: it took me a while to realize that 777 was the winning number on a slot machine. And I figured out that S.O.L. was poop out of luck (with another name for poop).

Thoughts taking root – yikes!

How could I move forward, expand my social circle, and experience more engagement with others? That question was something that stayed in my mind. A call from one of my best BYU friends, Laural, was just on time. I told her what was on my mind. She asked if I had ever thought about being a social worker because I was such a people person and a good listener. Wow, that was a nice surprise, but of course, it intensified my pondering.

So, I decided to pray about it and ask my Father in Heaven what I should do. I'm not an eloquent prayer, so I made it simple. It wasn't a comfortable ask because I didn't know if I was ready for the answer. It turned out to be a valid concern when I had a clear impression from Him that I needed to serve a full-time mission for The Church of Jesus Christ of Latter-Day Saints. Oh my, oh my, holy cow, were my stunned thoughts.

I cried and cried because serving a mission had never been in my plans, and this change in my life would be scary. Bill and Brenda Petty came to the rescue. My parents hugged me, heard me out, and understood my concerns. It was a direct answer to my prayers. And my mom encouraged me to acknowledge it was the Lord's Spirit answering me. Then my dad advised me to speak with the Bishop and express my concerns. He said, *"Keep praying and see how you feel as you progress with the mission application. If it's right, you'll know it."*

Thoughts on steroids

I made an appointment with Bishop Packer. He was over my California ward, and I was home for the summer. I sat nervously in the hall waiting. Of course, my mind was full of swirling possibilities of what may be to come.

When it was my turn, I felt somehow comfortable. I knew exactly what I was there for, and I needed some counseling.

It was a warm welcome as I stepped into his office. After a few updates and cordiality, Bishop Packer turned directly to me and said he could see something was on my mind.

I was very clear in what I was thinking and the answer I'd received to my prayer. He was very confident in somehow backing up my Dad's advice. Bishop Packer did produce a packet of application papers, which he laid on the desk. Then he mentioned a caveat in this process.

"Rachel," he said, "I'm sure it's no surprise that being endowed in the temple is something that you need to take care of before serving a mission." I nodded in agreement but was surprised by his serious tone in what came next. He said receiving your endowment is a gift from Heavenly Father, which includes sacred covenants that bind you to Him. It's an eternal promise that will connect you to your parents and future children. Wow, that got my thoughts percolating.

I continued to nod with my eyebrows up. "So, it's independent of and more important than serving a mission," I said. He slapped his desk with enthusiasm and gave me a loud "Exactly!" cheer with a thumb up.

It all felt so right! I told Bishop Packer what decision I was making and took the papers. Now, I was a woman with a purpose. It all clicked and confirmed the answer to my prayers. I knew exactly what I needed to do now to make it happen.

Happy day in the Petty home!

My parents and siblings were somehow very available when I came home. There was no need to keep them in suspense. I smiled widely and flashed my mission application forms. We all cheered. Having their love and support was great!

We talked about scheduling and a poll to see where everyone thought I'd go. I mentioned the conversation I'd had with Mr. Rasmussen and the fact that I'd keep working until leaving on my mission. Also, after finding out where I would serve, I would use my employee discount to buy clothes that would work in that climate.

"Wow, Rachel, you've been having some inspiration of your own!" said my Dad. "Good thinking!"

Making the doctor and dentist appointments to complete my pre-mission requirements went well. Then I had to fill out my mission application with the Church. There were questions about my openness to living abroad, my language ability, and more details. An essay about me was also required. It was so profound to me how automatic and logical every step came along. It felt right.

The physical appointments were done without a problem. Then my appointments with Bishop Packer and Stake President Varge Christensen were wonderful. My application was submitted to the Church within a month of my first appointment with the Bishop!

Oh, the waiting! My family circulated a poll where they guessed one domestic and one foreign mission. But no one chose correctly, which was interesting.

Peanut gallery responds

After telling my BYU friends that I was going to serve a mission, their response was very reassuring. A few of my girlfriends had even made the same decision! Our guy friends were also positive, and I appreciated their support. This was a great transitional time to swap contact information and make sure we kept in touch.

At first, we didn't know where we were being called. We encouraged each other and chatted via email, text, or calls. It was an exciting and suspenseful time as we all awaited our calls.

There were some who were surprised. They thought I would wait to get married. That was almost offensive. They apparently didn't think I was strong or capable enough to make that decision on my own, let alone do it.

I even told my fragrance & beauty non-friend about my mission decision. It wasn't a hard eye-roll, but she smirked and said, "You would." I told her the real name of the Church was the Church of Jesus Christ of Latter-Day Saints. She was a captive audience, so I further explained that we read The Book of Mormon, which is how we got the nickname "Mormon."

I even went on to explain the reason I changed to working full-time was to have enough money to pay for my mission. Her eyebrows shot up, and she blurted out, "They don't pay for you to go? You pay for it yourself?!" I confirmed, "Yes, that's what we do."

Not wanting to push it, I told her that I didn't know where I was going to serve. I then asked if she could recommend a good facial sunscreen. The ball was in her court now. She relaxed and became professional. It was very helpful getting her suggestions. After that, the ice was broken between us.

Now, the word spread in my local congregation that I had

decided to serve a mission. Most people were very supportive and said I'd do a great job. I received lots of tips and encouragement. However, some of the Young Men told me I shouldn't go because only "ugly chicks" served missions. What boneheads.

Amazing temple experience

The next step was attending the temple to receive my endowment. This was new for me. However, I was very focused on moving forward in my faith and testimony in Heavenly Father and His Son, Jesus Christ.

The Los Angeles Temple was my nearest. This beautiful temple has the profound inscription saying, "Holiness to the Lord: The House of the Lord," on the front wall. That same inscription is on all temples throughout the world.

The peace inside the temple was distinctly like no other. It was new and somewhat overwhelming, but I was comfortable because there were no different or awkward principles being presented. Nothing was outside the Gospel I studied personally, with family, and at church. However, beyond that, making personal covenants with God hit differently.

I had a new and confirmed identity as a daughter of Heavenly Father. Knowing that applies to every male and female was inspiring. The obvious epiphany that we're all God's children was a recalibration of my personal thoughts. Serving a mission was going to be awesome because I knew exactly who I would be helping.

The bus stop

Wondering where I was going was a trial. I felt like I was waiting at a bus stop with no idea where the bus was going and what time it would leave.

The shots for international travel were a painful must, and I also had my USA passport.

Then, I made sure I had pajamas, sufficient undergarments, basic tops, skirts, two of the family suitcases, and a good pair of walking shoes. That's about as bare minimum as it gets when traveling to an unknown location.

Some of my BYU friends had started getting their calls, and I was sure mine would come soon. I was nervous, as anyone facing the complete unknown is.

The Rollercoaster Ride Begins

I like riding roller coasters. The curves back and forth start the ride, and the expected incline begins. I was at the ride's peak now and knew the rapid swoosh down was coming.

My call to the Uruguay, Montevideo mission was a good surprise. It's over 6,000 miles away from Los Angeles, and I'd be speaking Spanish. Simple facts, but I was relieved I didn't have to learn a language with a different alphabet. And the fact I'd be leaving at the start of winter and going to summer in the southern hemisphere was amazing. However, humidity was a new beast I would need to tackle.

Our trip to the mall with my Mom was so much fun. We researched the best clothes to take to Uruguay. I would need cotton and lightweight clothes for hot months and synthetic and wool clothes for the cold. Having a Jekyll-and-Hyde wardrobe seemed unnecessary, but oh, how important it was to be prepared!

We stopped by the beauty department and visited my new friend Rita. I told her my call was to Uruguay and I would need sunscreen for my arms and face. She nodded while pulling out my best options. She said she'd never want to live in a fourth-world country. I smiled and told her I'd let her know how it was.

Then she asked me what my name was. I told her it was Rachel and introduced my Mom, Brenda. We had a nice get-to-know-you conversation. Then everyone laughed when I confessed that I'd only known her name because of her name tag. My Mom told Rita she'd keep her up to date on me when she was in the mall.

We used my employee discount to load up on missionary gear. As always, it was nice having time alone with my Mom. Purchases aside, retail therapy is a legitimate way to chat and bond.

The Rubber Hits the Road

Missionaries for The Church of Jesus Christ of Latter-Day Saints generally speak in their local congregation's Sacrament meeting the Sunday before leaving for their missions. So, my time was up, and while not being a polished public speaker, I did my best.

Bishop Packer and President Christensen were complimentary, and lots of supportive family members were also in attendance. My sweet Great Aunt Florence even came—she's a pistol! She repeated her common life advice motto to help me: "Don't compare, don't complain, don't contend, and don't criticize" was her well-rehearsed pitch.

I really appreciated everyone's support. That week, I flew to Salt Lake City, where I took the shuttle down to the Missionary Training Center in Provo, Utah. Yes, I'd lived there as a student, but entering the MTC was surreal.

We new missionaries were ushered into a room for our orientation. They explained how every detail would go, from our housing, eating, and training meetings. Of course, we had our badges on and were informed who our companions would be. I was somewhat fortunate to have Hermana (Sister) Miller from Jacksonville, Florida. I didn't know if we were two peas in a pod yet, but so far, so good. She was going to the Vina del Mar, Chile mission.

To be honest, I missed my regular life without someone by my side 24/7. It was a great, positive atmosphere with lots of smiles, but that would truthfully take some getting used to. I had to combine my capability with my creativity and sense of humor to make things go as successfully as possible.

It was like a Los Angeles Unified School District integration flashback putting strangers together. On the bright side, we shared the same beliefs and purpose. This was a mere glimpse of what was coming my way.

For almost two months, we learned Spanish using the "usted" form only, which is the formal, respectful way to speak. The "tú" form was to be spoken to children or animals. (Spoiler alert!) Those grammar rules did not apply to Uruguay.

We had spiritual devotionals focusing on Jesus Christ and learned guidelines for safety. On departure day, we were dressed, packed, and placed in flight groups with a designated travel leader. It was the second-to-last longest trip ever. My flight home was longer—yikes!

We flew from Salt Lake City International Airport to Chicago's O'Hare. It was life-changing to be out of the MTC's cocoon. All of a sudden, people were staring and curious about this clean-cut group wearing badges. Mine said Hermana Petty, La Iglesia de Jesucristo de Los Santos de los Últimos Días—aka Sister Petty, The Church of Jesus Christ of Latter-Day Saints. I was the freak now.

I was happy and pleased to be part of this "team." We were going out to serve others and teach those wanting to learn about the Gospel of Jesus Christ. We had no other agenda, and it was a good pursuit. However, I was very aware that I didn't blend in and was experiencing a completely new atmosphere.

After leaving Salt Lake, we flew to Chicago, Chicago to Miami, then to Peru, then to Buenos Aires, and finally to Montevideo, Uruguay. Our flights totaled over 24 hours. We arrived like limp noodles and tried to match our Mission President Ayala and his wife Blanca's cheerful smiles.

Here We Go!

This book was never meant to be a play-by-play of my mission. I wrote this with the original premise of what I was seeing and how I was being seen.

I'll start with the people aspect. The Uruguayan people are very nice and straightforward. If you're fat, they call you fat. If you're thin, they call you thin. This is without being insulting because it's just their culture. They're very perceptive as well. When the mother of the house saw me wincing at a bowl of "mondongo" (aka tripe), she told me I didn't have to eat it. Phew.

They were surprised that I was from California, not "the factory." They called Utah "la factoría" because the majority of missionaries come from there. Then, when I told them I didn't personally really know any TV or movie stars, they were disappointed.

There were some other surprising conversations. Like, "Yes, we do have flies in California. And oranges are grown there." One man insisted California was known for growing delicious apples, and I gave him the win. That was an argument I didn't pursue because I'm sure some apples are grown in California somewhere.

A very distinct fact about the Uruguayans is their lack of indigenous people. The majority of their population migrated from Europe due to World War Two. Yes, many of the people are brown-eyed and look Italian or Spanish, but almost as many were blue- or green-eyed with brown or blonde hair. One of my District Leaders was Carlos Hofmann, and he was a blonde, blue-eyed Argentine.

They eat mainly German or Italian food. There are no tacos or burritos—in other words, no Mexican food. Many assume that south of the border would include that cuisine. Only a few people knew that lots of gringos like spicy food.

One standout factor in Uruguay surprised me. They have ranches well outside town and raise beef. It was intriguing to me that there were cowboys, or "gauchos," who provided the butchers with fresh meat to cut and sell. We never walked that far out and never met them. But each town center had long rectangular barbecue grills selling the steaks.

Their desserts didn't disappoint, and their bakeries were impressive. Many of their cafes or bodegas looked European. Our strip malls and fast food restaurants in the U.S. are more commercialized and completely different from what I saw there.

Face to Face

My first companion, Hermana Mejia, was from Argentina. She had a Rita (Beauty & Fragrance coworker) vibe, surprisingly. I realized her living with someone from the United States of America was uncomfortable. She was very pretty and observed me and what I said daily.

When we had a missionary meeting, she would remind me not to talk to the Elders too much because it would look like I was flirting. Say what?! I had no intention of having anything romantic start up. That was not what I was there for.

One day, we were walking by a shop and I said that we should talk to the people there. I was fresh from the MTC with enthusiasm but wasn't speaking Spanish that well yet. She prompted me to go ahead and try, and that she would help me if needed. Oh boy, I thought she was supposed to be the one taking the lead.

Every companion would take some getting used to, no matter where they were from. An interesting thing was the difference in senses of humor between those from the USA and those from South America. I would say something that I thought was really funny and get a blank look in response. Dang, to me that was a good one!

Another tell-tale sign that I wasn't in a first-world country anymore was in the bathroom. I was surprised to see an "e" on my toilet paper. Apparently, newspapers were used for more than reading there. Also, using a squeegee on the shower walls was necessary to avoid mold from growing.

The humidity was hard but possible to live with. I had never sweated so much when it was hot. And when it was hot and as "dry" as possible, we would wash our sweaty clothes in the bathroom sink and hang them to dry. Fun fact: most homes in Uruguay have flat roofs, which were used like we in the USA use backyards. What an experience to sling wet laundry over my shoulder and climb a ladder to hang it on the roof's clotheslines.

Uruguay in the winter was hard to take, like anyone who lives in a humid climate knows. We didn't have a car or bicycle and wore skirts. Brrr! I doubled my tights, shirts, sweaters, and jackets or coat. I dressed like a bag woman to keep as warm as possible. And our apartments didn't have much insulation. So, I layered up as many sheets and blankets and used my coat like a tent over my head.

I learned the Uruguayans had pride and valued education. They would correct me when I said that I was an American. "We're Americans too," they'd say! Of course, we were from North America or South America. I couldn't claim that title without the caveat of which continent I was referring to.

The students wore uniforms there. That explained why people were asking me if I was going to class when I was wearing my navy-blue jumper dress with a white shirt. Their uniforms were just like what I was wearing. Who knew?

Our differences were null and unimportant when everyone felt they were treated with dignity and respect. The cherry on top was how nice the Uruguayans were. I had a quality international experience there.

Money Talks, One Way or the Other

Not too far into my time in Uruguay, we were walking. On one of the common dirt roads, a little, unkempt old woman approached asking for money. I was shocked when Hermana Mejia started to try shooing her away. I went fishing in my pockets and gave her the few coins I had found.

The woman said she just wanted to buy bones from the butcher to flavor her soup.

The woman hugged me and thanked me over and over again. In Uruguay, it's tradition to touch cheeks and make a kissing noise. It was hard and surprising to see the disgusted look on my companion's face. I reassured her that it was no big deal and that I didn't give her much. But I was astounded that the little gesture of sharing my change could mean so much.

This is where I started seeing the difference in people there. They treated each other well. There was no caste system, and poor people were generally not shunned. The difference in their clothes and homes showed their standing. Some of their homes had dirt floors with chickens walking about. Others had tile floors, and a very few had rugs or carpet. Chandeliers were never fully installed with light bulbs. They would save on electricity by not using all the lights.

The most impoverished used old tin cans as cups to drink from. They repurposed many things as a matter of course due to the lack of anything else. These residents were accommodated as well as possible in government housing projects. One old couple was very sweet and lived in one of these city project neighborhoods. Their front door didn't fit the front wall's opening. They were practical and propped the door up against the opening as best they could. There was nothing nice or new in their home.

The Uruguayans were aware of the variety of people around them, but generally showed congeniality in their interactions.

However, I was guilty of showing prejudice one day when a man with sloppy hair and attire was coming our way on the street. I nudged my companion to go towards the other side when the man came straight towards us. He greeted us with a smile and spoke in perfect English and was very nice! I had misjudged everything about him. It was a brief conversation, but I learned so very much.

One of the worst mistreatments I saw while on my mission has never left me. My companion and I had to take a bus for a meeting in another town. We stopped for something to eat. As we finished our lunch, a little club-footed boy hobbled in to beg. The café owner promptly came in shouting and telling the defeated little boy to get out and never come back. I was shocked and could have given him a little money. But it happened so quickly, he had scurried away and I was heartbroken. I immediately thought how simply he could have been treated and helped in the U.S. In Uruguay their healthcare at that time was subpar.

My thoughts evolved into this poem:

The nights are long for those who weep. For those who shiver in the street.

Or, in a house – dim, bare, small.

A cement box with tear-stained walls.

The children leave to stay alive.

They peddle, they beg, they hurt inside. A life of dread of hunger, scorn.

The worldly worries on their shoulders born.

—And trudge back whistling a shadowy song. For some poor kids, The nights are long.

Habla what?

Being coached to use the formal form of conversational Spanish was the first mistake in Uruguay. Even using the 'tú' form was looked down upon. They use the 'voseo,' and it sounded like Italian! The Spanish in Uruguay was sing-songy, and I was stunned. Why did no one tell us about this?

With my companion and the entire first district speaking only Castellano (what they call Spanish), I would go to bed with a headache. I was trying so hard to understand what was going on—it was frustrating!

Another kicker was that the double L's in Uruguay are pronounced like soft 'sh,' or a hard one, depending on the person. It took me a long while to realize that our friend's name, pronounced like 'Wee-sh-ahm,' was William! But, of course, the double L would be pronounced that way.

William Oxley was his name, and his wife Elizabeth had blue eyes and brown hair! The differences never stopped coming up, and I loved it.

I insulted some men as I learned the lingo and way of speaking. For example, we went to the market when we were first shopping for some groceries. I used my 'voseo' and thought it was accurate. However, the man selling eggs had an insulted look on his face. I was confused and pointed to the eggs and asked him if he had any eggs. Only later did it dawn on me that I was somehow questioning his masculinity. Oops!

Another very surprising discovery happened in another of my areas, Paysandú. As we walked through the community, I could hear that they weren't speaking Spanish. I was familiar enough with German that I realized that's what they were speaking. This was a Lutheran community speaking their original language!

Of course, my Spanish classes in school hadn't taught me how to have a legit conversation. My Spanish-speaking friends growing up had warned me which words I shouldn't say, which helped. The Church's missionary program is inspired. Their amazingly successful language education prepared me to speak Spanish (after a few months of getting used to the culture and lingo). I have friends and family members who now speak Portuguese, Marshallese, Mandarin, Japanese, and more because of that language program.

I learned Spanish well, and after my mission, I had some new realizations. While speaking with the Mexicans, Puerto Ricans, those from the Dominican Republic, and others, they didn't like hearing my Uruguayan pronunciation. My own sister, Jennifer, served her mission in Chile. She was somewhat disgusted by how I spoke. She said, "Oh no, you sound like an Argentine!" That was a prejudice or dislike I hadn't expected.

Wrapping Things Up

As I was close to finishing my mission, I had to think through a game plan of what was coming next. Summing up an eighteen-month mission is challenging. I left out details like the tarantulas in the room, snakes along the walking paths, and the man grabbing my arm as we walked by.

Everyone knows there are many details in a week, let alone months.

However, I had to get realistic about my return home. My thoughts swirled as we walked and walked and walked to and from meetings and appointments. Truthfully, I sometimes resented airplanes flying above and would discreetly roll my eyes and stick out my tongue. I was envious of their speed and freedom.

And after many denials and tiring days, I'd think, "I'd rather be home sweeping." That was a surprisingly specific thought, and I chuckled. Like I said, having a sense of humor was an important tool. And I'd remember my awesome Dad's sage advice: "Don't take yourself too seriously."

Classes in world history, humanities, sociology, and psychology became very attractive to me as I looked at the class schedule. What jobs would those classes prepare me for? My sweet Mom was my class schedule contact, and we arranged my next semester at BYU.

I thought about taking the Spanish proficiency exam when I got back on campus. I wanted to double major in sociology and Spanish. That would be a serious step forward and show my aim and purpose. My friend Laural had sparked a thought in my mind about being a social worker over a year earlier. And after living with a whole other community speaking a different language, that cemented my decision.

Hasta la Vista, My Friends

I dug in to finish my mission well. The needs of others and opportunities to be of service had been my focus during my whole mission. It paid off because my final interview with President Ayala was comforting and enlightening. He asked, "Hermana Petty, who can I assign our difficult sisters to without you?" What?! I hadn't realized those difficult companionships were on purpose. My freak/non-freak review was vaguely in the back of my mind, but I had come to realize the importance of differences.

Finishing up my mission was so much harder than I had anticipated. How can you say goodbye to people and a country you had worked with and grown to love so deeply?

When telling people I was going home, there was always a moment of disbelief. But they were aware that the missionaries were not there permanently. A discussion of how we were each feeling and how we would keep in touch followed. I had been a missionary for eighteen months, and the feeling of disbelief lingered.

Of course, I was looking forward to seeing my family because they were a great source of support. Their letters were touching, and the care packages went from delicious to hilarious. After I told them I had heat rash due to the humidity and moisture from sweating so much, Suzanne sent me a package with candy and diaper rash cream. Ha ha, it actually worked!

Bottom line: my belief in Jesus Christ as the world's Savior had been deeply strengthened. This happened when you teach about Heavenly Father's gospel and bear witness to friends. I'll never regret serving a full-time mission for The Church of Jesus Christ of Latter-Day Saints. It deeply rooted my strength and ambition to pursue the truths of the Gospel because of its benign beauty.

Hasta Luego, Uruguay!

The final pack-up for those of us returning went well, and we loaded into the mission van. We rode to the airport and boarded the plane. After lifting off from the tarmac, I broke into tears and cried and cried. That was something I hadn't expected. The feeling of heartbreak and loss was so strong. Working, teaching, and serving these new dear friends resulted in a deeper love than I'd ever known. My mission experience left me as someone with more substance or gravitas.

The trip wasn't easy. We flew into Miami, where everyone speaks Spanish, which was fine. I was thinking and dreaming in Spanish now. But, put on the brakes! My flight to Los Angeles was canceled. All of my friends from Utah boarded and took off for their flight to Salt Lake City.

There I was, alone! I hadn't been alone for a year and a half. The bathroom had been my only little area of retreat. But my alone time didn't last very long. A man from Peru sat next to me, trying to practice his English. Yikes! I was struggling to put my words and sentences together in English. He asked me if I spoke English with a doubting and furrowed brow.

I explained that I had been speaking about Jesus Christ and His gospel for over a year. That softened him up, and I was glad when he became more patient and understanding. I couldn't believe it when he asked if I spoke English. Oh boy, of course I did, but it was a clumsy conversation. I explained that I was a missionary for The Church of Jesus Christ of Latter-Day Saints, and that's why my non-religious words weren't coming easily. We ended as friends and wished each other well when it was time to part ways.

Mission Accomplished – Almost

Finishing my mission was very satisfying. I completed something difficult and have never regretted serving my mission. I can socialize with a variety of people; I can speak another language, and I have sharpened my focus to serve and do well. I have never been such a strong believer in Jesus Christ and still want to share that belief.

This new social understanding was suddenly tested when my friend Trina called me the very next day after I flew back home. It was great talking to her. We were in the same ward and played on our high school softball team together. She told me that she was living in Long Beach with her girlfriend. She then encouraged me to come join them and move there.

"You poor kid, having an upbringing that was so restrictive must have been hard!" started Trina. "And you being the Bishop's daughter for so many years would've been so tough. We would have a good time if you moved closer to the beach with us."

"Poor kid? Trina, we're the same age, and you know my parents!" I replied. "They were never oppressive or mean! Yes, we had rules, but they let us make our own decisions."

Our conversation stopped cold when I told her where I had just come back from. She automatically knew we had two very separate points of view. Homosexuality is something I'll never adopt. But years earlier, another friend, Brigitte, explained her decision to 'come out of the closet' when she could see and feel the understanding and caring between women. That's why she chose that lifestyle. I appreciated that opinion because it deepened the ease and understanding of our differences.

Getting ready to launch

There were four months before school began, and my family and I made the most of the time. I researched housing, employment, and the spectrum of careers possible in the social work field. Plus, my family and I had a great time together.

And, as a tradition, I gave my "homecoming" talk in Sacrament meeting. My first time speaking was with our local Spanish ward, which I loved because that's the language I had grown to love. Some of the ward members even told me that my Spanish was better than theirs! That was flattering, and it felt good.

During that four-month time, all of us Petty women went shopping. That was a blast, and my sisters updated me on the shorter hemlines that were in style. I pushed back but made some nice purchases for my next year of college.

I was pleasantly surprised that my Beauty and Health co-worker, Rita, was still working there. Her badge had the title of Department Manager, and I congratulated her on the promotion. It was fun to introduce my sisters to her, and she checked out our group.

My Mom said, "You know me, Rita! Brenda, Rachel's Mom!" She nodded and smiled. That's when I presented the novelty postcard from Uruguay to her, with my phone number on the back.

"Rita, it was a terrific experience and was more third world, not fourth world, and the people were the best!" I called out. She gazed at the postcard's photos and was interested. "If you have any questions, please let me know—my number is on the back." I hadn't had time or interest in turning down my missionary enthusiasm. My sisters smiled and looked at me with a questioning look about my fourth-world comment.

Now, I felt ready to pack up and return to my student life. I was excited for this next chapter in my life!

What comes around goes around – here I come!

Gearing up for my next year at BYU somehow felt like a great surprise. I was excited for my new study direction and possible career opportunities coming my way. It was like waiting for my mission call. I didn't know exactly what to expect, but somehow I had an unexplained, optimistic enthusiasm for this new school year. Being at the bus stop can be entertaining.

At this point, dating and possible freak encounters were a non-factor. They were like the weather, where predictions and forecasts could be made but not guaranteed.

My new apartment was like the U.N. I had served my mission speaking Spanish in Uruguay. Kathy served her mission in Germany and spoke German. Julie and Theresa served in Hong Kong and spoke Mandarin. My roommate Veronica was Italian but also spoke perfect French and English. Joan was our little outsider, non-missionary. She later ended up serving her mission in Peru.

It was a fun time cooking for each other and sharing our exotic entrees. My Uruguayan gnocchi were a favorite. We loved the Chinese food Julie and Theresa treated us to. Kathy's German schnitzel was delicious, but we did ask her to work on leaving the dish brush as cheese-free as possible.

Roll call!

My first class was Psychology 101, which was so interesting. I didn't tell my professor about my exclusive freak/non-freak experience, of course. It was the first time I'd taken a class about how we think, which was very thought-provoking. I realized I could be defined as a meta-thinker because I do think about what I'm thinking—or the thoughts of others. I'm an equal-opportunity thought reviewer.

I took Spanish 301 per the results on my post-mission assessment. It was so interesting to talk with other students who had mostly done as I had. We chatted about where we had served, and I bragged about Uruguay's Castellano being the best. The camaraderie was fun, and I appreciated being able to deepen my Spanish language skills. It would help in moving forward.

I chose an Old Testament class to fulfill my religion credit. Yes, I'd served a mission, but I knew there was always more to learn. As always, I enjoyed new people, new curriculum, and more information.

Now, sociology was a class that hit different because I had just been entrenched in living and working with many people and their unique cultures. Plus, I was studying about me—a regular human being. I was excited to focus on the lens through which I see people. There were a multitude of workshops connected to sociology, and I started researching the options being offered.

This was a life change I could sink my teeth into. I had never been so ready to dive into a new field of study. Weight lifting was an almost comical physical fitness choice, but it was a great class, and I learned important information about the conditioning and strengthening of muscles. That knowledge helped me as I moved forward in my additional classes.

Snow ball effect

Being so enthusiastic about my classes in the first half of the year was very exciting. This was great in a new way. The ideas of possible future career paths were firming up, so my class choices for the second half of the year were chosen confidently. I chose higher-level classes in Spanish, Religion, and Psychology. Humanities 101 was intriguing to me because it would include some world history.

An unexpected change came when my friend, Marcy, told me about a part-time job I might like. She knew my new interest in international concerns and social work. It was a call center job at a new airline needing bilingual agents. Robin Airways was local and ramping up quickly. It sounded like it would be worth a try, and it included flight benefits—yay! So, I interviewed with them and was hired quickly.

My class and work schedules were a good fit, and I looked forward to the combination. It was a busy and educational semester. One project I loved in my Psychology class was an assignment to dress down one day, and then dress up on another. It wasn't a dirty or grunge look Dr. Magleby wanted, but a very casual, simple outfit without jewelry, scarves, or any hair improvements.

That was a fascinating day. I wasn't standing tall or feeling confident because I knew I wasn't looking my best. Observing others was my task. It was very obvious that those passing by as I walked through the hallways were not making eye contact with me. No one really noticed me somehow. I was easy to ignore.

The day I dressed nicely with perfect makeup and hair was a revelation. My confidence was much better, and I walked with my head up. I looked around as I went about my day and noticed others watching and smiling at me. Wow, that was an easy way to attract attention! Lesson learned.

It reminded me of that day on my mission when I avoided walking close to that sloppy man—yes, that man who spoke perfect English and was very nice. The class project mentally cemented this experiment in my memory, I thought.

Thanks for calling Robin Airways!

My new job was so interesting. The two-week training was quick and intense. We were taught their call protocol with customers. The computer programs needed to be learned piled on more important information. Learning to take payments was more detailed than I had expected.

I liked that job and learned excellent customer service. The cherry on top was learning of a Conflict Resolution Official training being offered. Every airline and airport is required to have at least one CRO on duty. And I wanted to learn about as many experiences as people are exposed to when they travel. Plus, any credentials that may help me as a social worker would be beneficial.

That CRO training was more intense than that of the customer service agent. We learned how to lift people up and transport them in wheelchairs or carts. They taught us how to transfer passengers in and out of the plane. There were many calls from upset family members whose loved ones had been wronged.

For example, an elderly woman's reservation clearly stated LANG, showing she had speaking limitations in English. Because she knew only Spanish, she missed her connecting flight. Our crew had failed to meet and assist her. I was able to accommodate her family's complaints and assure her safe return home. The CRO calls helped me feel capable and satisfied in my ability to help.

Another education I received was working at the call center was just talking to people from all over the world. There are so many accents in English and Spanish. That was a fun observation because it brought me a deepened realization of how unique people really are.

One call still makes me laugh. I answered a call and helped a man with a nasal-y, deep voice—maybe from Minnesota or

Michigan? We talked, and I helped figure out what was needed.

He then slowly said, "Hmm, well…I don't want to be rude … it's not like you're an alien or anything … but you sound good!" This man had apparently never been west of the Mississippi. My regular Californian accent was something unique and special to him. That was, and is still, funny. Of course, I don't think I have an accent. I just speak normally, right? It all depends on where you come from.

There's one last example or question that comes to mind. How on earth do the U.S. New Englanders or the British teach their kids how to read? It can't be with the phonics program. Their 'R's are a mere soft placeholder. Departed is 'depahted' and really, somehow, has a 'W.' That can be quite a discussion, but I'll get off my soapbox.

Moving forward

This third school year was great because I had a purpose. Psychology and social work became my focus, but I knew more education and experience were needed. This new energy toward an area that would shape my future career was exhilarating. I dug in and learned everything I could about the options available.

I had been dating, going to dances, of course, and enjoying the football games. To be honest, none of the guys I dated sparked any romantic feelings. They were great guys, and I'm glad we're now friends, but you can't make something out of nothing.

The social work community groups were so helpful because they had a deeper understanding of everything included in becoming a social worker. I hadn't realized how many types of social work existed. The first two areas that appealed to me in a naïve way were shadowing jobs following qualified social workers in a junior high school and at the local hospital. Wow, what a wake-up that was!

Those two pursuits were gratefully combined in collaboration with my schedule. However, both areas were very difficult, as I learned in my first shadowing attempt. Junior high school students had a potpourri of emotions and real-life concerns.

I was an observer and could not counsel or offer options since I was unqualified and uncertified. It was surprising to me how many students used tattoos and piercings as personal fencing. I tended to ask if a specific tattoo was painful to get. It usually helped them to open up a little and expand on others. One thing holding me back, surprisingly, was my empathy. When people have critical problems and cry, I tend to join in. That, of course, is unprofessional, which my mentor confirmed.

Shadowing in the local hospital was no walk in the park. There was less conversation about the patient. Social work in the hospital tended to lean toward insurance coverage and how we could help there. However, there were cases of abuse and criminal misconduct that broke my heart.

Some police records came into play and were added to the patient's file.

To say I was out of my league was an understatement. Was I barking up the wrong tree? Dang, neither of those shadowing jobs was anything I'd like to have a career doing. Could I really have been that far off base on what I thought I wanted to do?

Mom and Dad to the rescue

A call home saved the day. It wasn't a quick-fix kind of conversation, but they listened carefully. I described my shadowing job attempts and how hard it was for me to be more professional than sympathetic. I had never been this quick to cry. But after meeting and working for so many weeks with new friends in Uruguay, my emotions had become closer to the surface.

Well, the apple doesn't fall far from the tree! My Dad wondered the same thing about possibly barking up the wrong tree. Then, my sweet Mom chimed in, suggesting I not throw the baby out with the bathwater. That got me thinking about the other social work courses being offered.

They asked what kind of alternatives I'd seen. I mentioned several and chuckled at the "Hands-on Equine Therapy" option, which took place at a local farm with an expert social worker. I had looked up "equine" and saw it had to do with horses. So, I would probably not be shedding sympathetic tears with them.

They asked me why he was called an expert, and I wasn't sure. Other students referred to Dr. B as the toughest, but best, professor and trainer in the field. Bill and Brenda jumped on that information. Why not try getting into Dr. B's class?

I countered with the fact that I'm far from a farm person. They came back, assuring me I wouldn't be milking the cows and that I should give it a try.

Why not? Little did I know my life was about to change.

Throwing the dice

I continued with my classes that semester and talked with the academic counselor about my upcoming course choices. I mentioned the "Hands-on Equine Therapy" class and asked if it really took place on a farm. She smiled, nodded, and gave me a business-like assessment.

"What!?" I asked. She then pulled out an application form, which totally blew my mind. "Is it hard to get into that class?" I asked.

She explained Dr. Bennion's approach to vetting his students. He had a stringent process to ensure each class member was a good fit. There was a group chat for those wanting to attend his five-credit class to explain its strenuous curriculum. I was nervous but signed up for the next available spot.

The initial meeting was surprisingly casual. We were asked to write out our farm experience. What the heck?! Like I said, I am no farm person. The others started writing quickly, like they had something to say. Oh boy, I checked and confirmed that I could turn my paper in later.

I got a few curious looks, but I was told I could submit it by the end of the week. Thank goodness! I had some explaining to do.

A City Girl's Confessions

Dear Dr. Bennion,

Here's my city girl background, which is obviously lacking farm work. I hope you can accept this, knowing that I love learning new things and working hard. Plus, I just finished serving my mission in Uruguay and speak Spanish now.

>I did grow up with cats and dogs at our home in California.

>We visited my Aunt Ruth and Uncle Evan's huge garden on vacation in Utah. Every plant looked beautiful so I gasped when my uncle reached down and pulled out a perfect and healthy specimen. He was pleased as he shook the extra soil off and announced what a great potato it was. Yikes! I hadn't known potatoes grew underground.

>The revelations continued when I started attending BYU. There were brown cylindrical things all over the grass. They must have had a dog show, and you would think the proud owners would clean up after their prized canines. I had never seen or known about aerating lawns.

>One day, no lie, I stopped a complete stranger and asked him what the red stuff on the mountain was. I pointed up to the mountain, as if he didn't know where it was. I had heard about a rivalry BYU had with the University of Utah, but didn't know if that was the reason for the color change.

The man said, "That's the trees!" I stupidly asked him the same question, and again he gave me the same answer - "they're trees!" Growing up for me, I guess fall was when the acorns and their lids came off the oak trees onto the sidewalks and crunched when you stepped on them.

>One time only, I offered to help my roommate's family, who lived nearby. They asked me to plant the tulips, which I thought was

a really cool thing to do for the first time. I thought the pointed side should be planted down so it could grow into the ground. Luckily, my friend's dad caught on to what I was doing and redirected my efforts to correct my mistake. I apologized and said we never planted tulips in California.

>The last one I'll mention is suggesting we go to Lagoon in November. I heard it was an amusement park and thought it would be fun. Disneyland never closes, so I was stunned when told it was closed during the winter. Another surprise I hadn't expected. Amusement parks in Utah don't close (except when the employees are in school and the temperatures are in the 30s and 40s – duh.)

I hope my confessions aren't a deal breaker because your class sounds fascinating. Thanks for your time and consideration. I look forward to meeting you and discussing my possible role as one of your students.

Thank you, Rachel Petty

I dropped my paper into Dr. Bennion's 'In' basket and held my breath.

Finals and new beginnings

Finals were tough at the semester's end, as normal. Non-college students can't understand how to cram all the details needed to pass their classes with good grades. Then again, I had enjoyed all my classes and was confident I'd do well.

That smugness evaporated a little when I checked my emails and saw one from Dr. Bennion. Was this a kind or back-handed way to inform me, an urban young woman like me should stay far away from anything connected to anything related to being equine?

Well, it was a simple, generic invitation to join the class at the farm. He explained his timing so as to meet us before we all went home for the holidays.

Very good, I didn't get kicked out! We in the Social Work group called each other to see who would be joining that class. I was surprised at the small group's enthusiasm I saw and nervous, but I always like to at least try new things.

BYU arranged a van for us as transportation to the farm. It took about forty-five minutes to get to the farm. We all jumped out and were directed to the barn. It was pretty clean, and one of the hired hands in his t-shirt/baseball cap/jean ensemble was using a pitchfork to gather up stray hay. We were all chatting when the worker stood up straight and turned towards his next task.

Dang, he was a little rough but very good-looking. I waved and said 'hi' because I didn't want to be rude. He hung his pitchfork on a wall hook and turned to the ropes needing arrangement. I raised my hand, stepped forward, and asked what I could do to help.

It was a night and day difference when he looked at me and smiled. "This is exactly why I have you come before the next semester starts", he said. "I just need to get a feel for the people I'll be working with." There were a few gasps and some whispers of

"Is this Dr. B.?" Everyone shuffled uncomfortably until the "farm hand" took control.

"Good morning, I hope everyone's doing well. It's time for introductions as we'll be working closely together," he stated. "I'll start, and my name is Dr. Frank Bennion, and I'm the "Professor" of this course," he said this with a smile and quick salute. "And just so you're sure, equine is pronounced 'eek-wine', not 'egg-wine'." There was a mutual nod, and I know I appreciated this clarification.

Dr. B. then asked us to go around and give our names and hometowns. That was a normal ask and proceeded normally with no big surprises because only two of us were from other countries. But when it was my turn, I drew lots of attention. Dr. B interrupted and asked me to confirm my name. Yes, I repeated my name was Rachel Petty. He didn't outright laugh, but shook his head with an almost smirk. My classmates looked at me curiously.

Oh no, he had read my "city girl confessions" and was pondering my therapy choice! He spoke again after clearing his throat thoroughly. Good country man, Dr. B. then explained that I didn't have a lot of farm experience. But, he continued, saying that the fact I was the only one who offered to help was the difference in working on a farm. Because of the variety of tasks on a farm, hard work in many areas is important.

I felt satisfied but didn't dare get cocky. Some of my fellow classmates were wearing cowboy hats and boots! Wow, I didn't own either and had just worn my Nikes.

He then blew my mind by saying his job is to train you, fine students, how to mediate between the horses and their patients. I swear he saw my eyes go as big as saucers with uncertainty. We were then directed into the farmhouse to watch a video of trained equine therapists working with veterans, the disabled, and people who had been abused with their therapy horses.

The therapists were so sweet, or I should say sensitive, when they shared the history of each horse and patient. They then matched each pair to suit their individual past stories and needs. This is how they achieved successful partnerships. This education was a lifesaver for me and my understanding. I felt like I was taking baby steps in getting my feet under me in this new venture.

Hands-on orientation

We met the next day again with those wanting additional instruction. There was already a friendly feeling in the group. Dr. B shocked me when he pointed at me and nodded his head, calling me 'Ginger'. What?! I had auburn hair, but it was surprising. Lots of others looked at me and smiled. I just shrugged my shoulders with a palms and eyebrows up posture. I didn't want it to seem like Dr. B and I had any special friendship.

However, truthfully, it tingled that he had paid me special notice. I couldn't help but smile. Some of the others gave me a nudge and a wink. It was enjoyable to have this fun camaraderie. Dr. B did mention that our tasks would fit our skills, and luckily, gardening wasn't one of the tasks he said with a laugh. Oh, so many questions were suddenly on the table. Maybe I should make my confessions public? People were chatting and wondering about what he was referring to, but that could wait.

The atmosphere thankfully changed when Dr. B suggested we walk out and meet the horses. Other farmhands had opened fences and let the horses meander around. I tiptoed around on the open ground, realizing I didn't know the correct farm terms. The fresh air was brisk and refreshing. I felt like I was cheating by watching what the others were doing.

I had never felt like such an apprentice, such a rookie, but I was intrigued by what I was learning. My pondering was interrupted by a hairy nose nuzzling my shoulder. Yuck! Was my first response, but when I turned and saw the horse's big brown eyes, it was a warm surprise. I reluctantly petted the caramel colored animal's neck. Some of the others were touching the noses of their new friends and being comfortable with the interaction.

It was extremely interesting to watch how we naturally paired up with the horse we felt safe with. But, truthfully, my horse was bigger than I thought I could handle. So, I timidly continued petting the horse.

That's when Dr. B showed up by my side, handing me a big grooming brush. He advised me to brush her hair until it looked tangle-free and smooth. That sounded doable and simple.

I took note of the horse's gender, as he had mentioned, and confirmed it with him. He said she was a good choice for me because she needed a gentle companion. It broke my heart when he continued with her history of being an abused and starved farm animal.

When we work with patients, matching the horse's history, the two can somehow relate. This was a delicious epiphany to me. It somehow clicked, and I really loved it.

What a step forward for me. I never imagined I would ever say, "It was a really good day at the farm."

Before we wrapped things up and made sure the horses were fed and corralled, Dr. B announced one on one training opportunity the next day. I was part of a small group of those interested. I was eager to take advantage of this option.

A little too close for comfort

We met at the parking lot the next morning to take the ride to the farm. There were just three of us. The other two were the foreign students from Spain and Argentina! Ay, we can speak Spanish!

We chatted on the drive and got along very well. Maria Santos was from Argentina, and Guillermo Aragon from Spain. I teased him because in Los Angeles, the nickname for Guillermo was Chewy.

The laughter continued when we got there and saw Dr. B's t-shirt. At first glance, I thought it had a pro-vegetarian/anti-carnivore message. The front of the shirt said, "Meat is murder!"   Then the back of the shirt said, "Tasty tasty murder."

I laughed so hard, it caught the others' attention. First, I realized Maria and Chewy didn't understand what it said until I translated it for them. They chuckled, but on my mission, I realized sense of humor doesn't always translate.

Dr. B joined us and gave me a 'high five'. He thanked me for making them feel more comfortable. He also suggested that I translate terms and ideas that they may not understand. He said that he served his mission in El Salvador, but didn't have Spanish as fresh as mine.

The horses we had chosen yesterday had already been brought out. Dr. B put his arm around my shoulders and headed with me towards Buttercup (that's what I named her). His closeness gave me the warm trembles. Does that make sense? It did to me because I felt them.

It was such a relief when Chewy asked Dr. B a question. I had begun noticing our professor's thick, dark brown hair and the fact that his brown eyes were the same color as mine. Yikes, how do you put the brakes on sudden puppy love?

Another gross natural relief came when good ol' Buttercup pooped. We all got a laugh at the timing. Dr. B turned the moment into the lesson's visual aid. He pointed out a practical lesson by saying that when they poop, just check on their tails. He said, "If they're swinging, take cover."

I learned so much that day. Then, I could check on their food and if they had enough water.   Being close to Buttercup also felt mutually comfortable. And, luckily I would have time to sort out what I was feeling for Dr. B. He didn't have a wedding ring on. That's a quick observation, but other than that, I didn't have a clue. I was going home for Christmas break and would enjoy what I had started and contemplate how it may turn out.

I wished Dr. B Merry Christmas and said I look forward to continuing his class in January. He nodded and said the same. He then added that he'd never met anyone like me and looked forward to further conversation about my confessions with a big smile on his face.

Ho Ho Woah!

Christmas break was so fun with my family. The gap of being gone on my mission and at BYU left lots of questions for my family. We talked for hours and enjoyed catching up on how everyone was doing.

They had many questions about the details of Uruguay. It was so nice to share our common beliefs and the questions we had. The open conversation was freeing and without judgment. I also loved their appreciation and understanding when I shared my special experiences.

I told them about my decision to learn about psychology and sociology. They asked me what I'd do with that. I reviewed with them about my experiences shadowing social workers in a junior high and the local hospital, which I didn't like.

Then, I told them about my Hands-on Equine Therapy class. Not surprisingly, there was a burst of laughter. 'Rachel, you're a total city girl!' more than one of them said. 'Are you sure?'

Well, the ace up my sleeve was mentioning my stellar professor, Dr. Frank Bennion. He's the best in that kind of therapy and knows what he's doing. Plus, my sympathetic tears will be easier to handle with a big horse cushion.

My spontaneous Dr. B commercial was interrupted when Jane shouted, "Wow! He's legit and very handsome." She and some others started looking him up on their laptops.

So, 'how's the student/professor relationship going?' they asked with a giggle. I caved and admitted that I didn't know Dr. B really well yet, but he gave me the tingles. Everyone burst out laughing when I said, 'Hmm, I guess I'd better make sure he's available.'

The inevitable questions about my sisters' romances were

going to come up. Suzanne was dating a great accountant whom she met at her work. Jennifer was still shopping for the right man. Then Jane surprised us all when she announced an escalation in the relationship she just started six months ago with Vincent.

Brenda announced a pause in the chat. She pleaded that we coordinate dates, locations, and colors if things were getting serious. My practical Dad suggested we all choose the same colors to make things simpler. This created more laughter and expert ideas.

Dad's wisdom comes through again

The next morning's breakfast gave me a wonderful opportunity to chat with my Dad. My Mom had made her delicious crepes. It turned out that we had some alone time before others came down to eat.

My Dad surprised me when he said my therapy choice sounded like a good fit for me. I was curious and asked why.

He pointed out how I'd always been able to read between the lines with people. That's a rare gift he'd noticed about me. What about my freak magnet problem? He said the third-party approach I would take between the horse and patient would give me time to ponder and assess the two. Okay, there's a solution, I thought.

I asked him if he'd experienced this in his life. He nodded, then described the death of his sweet grandma, Lilly. He said he was bawling as he drove and was shouting in disbelief. Didn't these other people realize what had just happened?!   They just drove by in ignorance of his piercing tragedy.

"This is where you come in," he said. "Your Mom was at work that day but knew I'd be with my grandma, who was receiving hospice care. When she got home just after I did and saw my face, she automatically burst into tears and hugged me tight."

He continued saying, "Rachel, your tears don't make you a weak person. You have a deep understanding of how people feel and can relate. Your Mom has that talent too, and that deepens my love for both of you! That's why I love the therapy you've chosen, you'll help lots of people."

Needless to say, we did some crying and hugging. My Dad wasn't generally someone who spoke openly about his feelings. So that conversation is something I'll remember forever. It was a confidence boost as well. And, who doesn't need a confidence boost?

Mall déjà vu

Later that day, we Petty women went to the mall. Retail therapy is a real thing, right? Plus, it was decided I needed some kind of boots for farm work. I refused cowboy boots because who was I kidding? I liked the boot idea with my LA Dodgers cap.

So, we found the perfect pair of suede high-top boots with a zipper. They were very comfortable, cute, and on sale. That's what we Petty women call a 'victory purchase!' We celebrated and chatted over a food court lunch.

They asked me about Dr. B, whom Jane had searched out online. She said he was a cowboy champion, a sheep rancher, an award-winning equine therapist, and from what she could see, unmarried.

I liked what I was hearing and told them the tingle was still there. We all giggled, and I changed the subject to Jane's Vincent. She smiled and said the tingles were there. He was funny, polite, and a real gentleman, she said. "Jane, you could be describing your favorite mechanic! Have you been on any good dates?" I asked.

We all laughed about our work-in-progress social lives. Then, Mom, we suggested going to the department store to try on some perfumes. It was one of our favorite mall traditions.

Upon entering, Rita was right there in the front! We smiled and started talking with her. I noticed the Assistant Manager title on her name badge. "Congratulations on your promotion, Rita!" I said. She smiled and nodded, saying, "It took a while, but I did it!"

We all congratulated her, and she asked about us. My Mom took the lead like moms tend to do when talking about their kids. She highlighted every one of us, then came to me, saying I was going to start studying Equine Therapy.

"That's awesome, Rachel!" Rita said loudly. "I have a Down

syndrome little brother who goes to that therapy!" She continued to rave about how much he loves it and how confident it makes him feel taking care of a horse.

I was overjoyed meeting someone who was familiar with equine therapy. We agreed to keep in touch about this and swapped phone numbers. She said she lost the Uruguay postcard I'd given her with my number.

"Have you been back to Paraguay?" she asked. I confirmed that I served my mission in Uruguay and learned to speak Spanish. I continued that no, I haven't been back, but someday I'd love to return.

Rita then turned to my sisters, asking if they'd served the mission. They replied one at a time. Suzanne had chosen not to serve a mission. Jennifer served her mission in Chile. Jane went to Tallahassee, Florida, on her mission.

"You all must love that church!" said Rita. We nodded 'yes' and almost unanimously asked, "Do you want to know more?" I was so impressed with Suzanne when she told Rita she was always available for questions or to go to church with her.

I chimed in, saying that The Church of Jesus Christ of Latter-Day Saints was something we loved because it teaches the gospel of Jesus Christ. But I was going back to school to learn more.

We all hugged and exchanged phone numbers with Rita. I knew the wheels were turning in her head. I let her know I wanted to keep up with her and her little brother. I then asked if I could call about him and how the equine therapy was going. She nodded with a smile on her face, and our mall trip was a great success.

Back to the farm

I was truthfully happy to be back at BYU. Yes, my hands-on Equine Therapy class with Dr. B was exciting because I had actually met someone seeing its benefits!

The second class for my Science credit, I enrolled in was Geology. That sounds boring, but in Utah, you can see the layers of rock formed in different time periods. Plus, there was so much for me to learn.

The Equine Therapy van was there to transport us to what felt like a different time. This working farm was just that and was very authentic. I had my new boots on with my Dodgers cap and felt like I fit in a little more.

My classmate, Garth, came in his full cowboy ensemble. He was wearing his Wrangler jeans; plaid button-up shirt, bright grass green bandana around his neck, perfect cowboy hat with a fancy feather tucked in the band, a belt with a shiny rodeo award buckle and multi-colored embroidered cowboy boots. Oh my. Dr. B heard me say under my breath 'guilty of flaunting it without having it' when Garth the peacock had strutted by. That cracked him up and he started laughing hard. I loved that our senses of humor seemed to sync.

Then, I mentioned that a friend's brother was having equine therapy.

I added that she loves it because he has Down syndrome, and it helps him feel confident when he takes care of his horse. Dr. B said he appreciated me telling him that.

I wasn't expecting what came next. When we were all gathered together, Dr. B said we would be starting real hands-on therapy with patients today! We were shocked. But our horses were out, and a mixed group of our patients started coming out the farmhouse's back door.

Seeing Buttercup coming my way was comforting. What we saw next made sense. Dr. B instructed the patients to walk around to meet the horses. It was exactly what we students did so we could assess our horse choices. Watching them maneuver around was an education in itself. We could see those who were comfortable, nervous, or just plain scared.

I watched those moving near my Buttercup and realized how protective I had already become. This feeling expanded to the young man burned from the side of his face and down his arms who moved more closely to our horse, our Buttercup.

With perfect timing, Dr. B advised us to move in slowly and look at the horses at the same speed as the patients. We did so and checked the responses of both of them. My guy was nervous, but somehow knew how to handle Buttercup. I had grabbed a brush because it was the only 'tool' I knew how to use.

I said 'hi' to my counterpart, but he wouldn't lift his eyes to me. I followed his lead and turned my attention to softly brushing the horse with my eyes down. It was a big surprise when my 'patient' said, "She's not a puppy."

I nodded and agreed, saying, "A puppy that big would scare the heck out of me!" Another surprise came when my new buddy let out a big laugh. It was the sweetest sound, and it made me smile because it was so genuine. This guy would be worth getting to know, of course.

"My name is Rachel," I said. He kept his head down and worked on Buttercup's perfect grooming. This was going well. So, I asked him his name. There was silence until he finally said, "My name is Alex."

From the first week to the cattle drive?!

With my rural therapy education taking so much time, going to my Geology 101 class was a nice change. It was a fascinating curriculum, and the professor, Dr. Smith, had a fun teaching approach. So, while I missed the farm and Dr. B, this was a great educational buffer zone. Plus, Dr. Smith was a solid decade older than me and wasn't my type.

He started by describing how Utah is a Geological treasure chest because there are so many features so easily visible. We studied the general rock types, formations, history, and so much more. I knew I had a whole new vocabulary to learn, but that's something I've always liked.

This would also be so interesting because I'll be outside so much more at the farm. I started reading right away, so I didn't get behind. Balancing Geology, Hands-on Therapy, and part-time work with Robin Air will be important to accomplish.

My forward thinking would pay off, because my first email after class was from Dr. B! Of course, it wasn't personally to me, but my feelings with him still caused a tingle. And, through tactful questioning, I confirmed that he's single!

That was exciting, until I read the last line of his email. We were going with our patients on a cattle drive! What the heck?! I'd become comfortable brushing Buttercup and listening to anything Alex said. But 'please don't tell me I need to saddle a horse' was my first thought!

Good thing I wasn't a pioneer!

Well, sure enough, a cattle drive was planned for the next week. Dr. B introduced the cattle drive by saying it would be a good way to strengthen the friendships with our patients. He was thorough about what it would include and where it would be, Fillmore, Utah. So, an hour-long van ride would give me a little time to tamp down my uncertainties.

My favorite (and only) John Wayne quote came to mind, so I said, "Courage is being scared to death…and saddling up anyway." I thought it appropriate to share with the group when we boarded the van heading to my first-ever cattle drive. I got a few thumbs up and a request to say it again from Dr. B.

Everyone in the van was chatting, so Dr. B changing seats to sit next to me didn't cause a stir in the others. But I was nervous and now very aware that he was sitting right next to me. He quietly asked if I was scared, and I nodded yes. Dang, he smelled good! It was the fresh out of the shower good, not the heavy pre-date cologne, and it made me smile.

He then said I would be very pleased to have Alex as my patient. No details were added, but he reassured me he would have my back. I nodded my head and said 'thanks.'

When we arrived at the cattle ranch, everything looked approachable, but I was cautious. My nerves started fizzing up when our students and horses arrived. We were directed to meet out in the field behind the farmhouse.

I felt so gratified and happy when Alex smiled when he saw me. Everyone walked to their partners. The meeting of the students, horses, and patients had a very comfortable feeling. I looked quickly to see if Buttercup was saddled and panicked to see she wasn't.

That's when Alex stepped in with a saddle and started showing me how to put it on. I complimented his skill with horses and asked if he was a cowboy. A shadow darkened his face as if an old memory cloud was blocking the light. We'll talk about it later, I said.

He quickly finished the task and motioned to help me up. With the help of a nearby crate, I easily stepped up and swung my leg over into the first stirrup. Alex smiled and positioned my foot into the next nearest stirrup. I reached down, patted his back, and said, "Thank you very much- Alex, you're the best!"

To my surprise, he got on a nearby horse and was ready to ride. Dr. B walked over to confirm we were all set. "Am I helping Alex, or is he my boss?" I asked. "A little of both," Dr. B chuckled. "You two are taking the lead going down Main Street all the way to the corrals."

Alex pointed his chin in the direction we needed to go, and we moved out. I laughed because riding the lead horse in a cattle drive was something I'd never dreamed of or wanted to do. We were a good team and rode for over half an hour until we reached the barn with the corrals.

Now we were all tasked with first keeping the cattle moving through the pathways.   (Is that what they're called? I wondered.) That first job was where we came in using sticks to prod the cows along. Thank goodness that's the job I had.

The next two tasks were branding and inoculating the livestock. That was much more physical, and the hot brands stunk. There are some things you don't know you don't know. This was a big herd, and I was keeping those cows in line.

They were just ambling on one in front of another. What came next was so gross! One cow pooped straight on the cow's head behind it. Neither the pooper nor the pooped upon even flinched; they just kept walking. They weren't very intelligent, and I came to a new belief in my life, which I proclaimed out loud.

"I will never feel badly about eating steak, beef jerky, or a hamburger again!! That's what these beasts were born for!" I shouted. The cherry on top of the cattle drive was hearing Alex laugh.

After riding back to the farm, there was more to learn. We were unsaddling our horses, cleaning up, and putting things back where they belonged. Just after cleaning off my boots, I stood up and suddenly felt something unexpectedly hit my nose!

I yelled out, "Hey!!! That hurt!" and dropped to my knees. Most people know that eye-watering pain after being hit in the nose. To make it worse, my nose was bleeding profusely.   My fellow cowboys caught on to what was happening and gathered around.

"What hit my nose?" I asked. People started handing me bandanas to stop the bleeding and clean me up.

"I'm so sorry, I knew the Frisbees went in the recreation bin and gave it a toss," said Brian. That bin had footballs, soccer balls, and obviously Frisbees to use for fun between chores.

Things calmed down when Dr. B joined the group and quickly assessed what had happened.

"Hey, Ginger, you okay?" asked Dr. B. I nodded yes, but my face was throbbing. He asked Chewy and Maria to get an ice pack and some kitchen towels.

His instructions were then very straightforward to throw things when those nearby or the recipients knew what was coming. Also, if you don't know where things go, ask.

Then, he helped me up and put his arm around me as we walked to the van. With that sweet gesture, I was feeling better already. And, he made sure I was seated comfortably.

Out of the farmhouse came someone I thought was another social worker or maybe a resident. He greeted her as 'Tami,' who was all smiles. She took Dr. B's arm. I had never seen her, and it looked like she liked him. No! This was the first time I had ever felt jealous of another woman.

Wow, I liked Dr. B and didn't want competition!

You should see the other guy!

My Geology class the next day was a 'true confessions' kind of experience because when Professor Smith and my classmates saw my double black eyes, they were curious and wanted answers. I told them I needed their help creating a dramatic or humorous answer, but the bottom line, a Frisbee I wasn't expecting had come my way yesterday.

It was the best class ever. It turns out black eyes are a real ice breaker. We suddenly got to know each other better.   And their sense of humor was hilarious. Even Professor Smith chimed in with a microscopic meteor shower idea. He said that NASA officials were on their way to assess my injury and situation.

It was the funniest class ever. We learned about the first sedentary rock formations and where they can be found in Utah. The class went on with a long lecture on how the different layers were formed and their timeline.

It wasn't fun and games when Dr. Smith reminded us to keep studying the textbook as we moved along in class, because that's where the midterm questions come from.

When class was over, my classmates and professor came up with funny nicknames for me. Professor Smith called me Rocky, and others called out 'Bruiser', 'Sugar Ray', and 'Mohammed Ali'. Good times for the injured – ha ha.

Back in the saddle

After the experience in my Geology class, I knew how going back to my Hands-On Equine therapy class would probably play out. And yes, there were multiple eyeballs focused on me when we gathered.   There were hugs and pats on my back from the others.

When Dr. B came in, he had a shocked look and said, "Double black eyes?! Wow - sorry about that, Ginger."   He asked if I was all right to ride, and I said yes with more confidence than I really had.

What surprised me was Alex's reaction when our patients arrived. He looked truly concerned when he saw me. The surprise continued when he said, "Rachel, are you all right? Are you going to be okay?"

I walked slowly over to him and assured him I would be all right. We then saddled up and got on our horses. Per Dr. B's direction, we went on a slow ride. Alex and I took a slow amble side by side.

Alex told me how everybody asks him how he was burned. I held off saying anything to see if he would keep talking. He did, and continued by saying, "It was spontaneous combustion in our barn."

"My goodness, it's a good thing you're so tough, Alex," I said. "Wow, I didn't know how that could happen." I wasn't sure if we should compliment our patients or just treat them like friends. That's a conversation I would have to have with Dr. B.

We headed back to the farm without saying much. I did ask him if he grew up with horses, because he seemed to know exactly what to do with them. Alex nodded yes, and we returned to the farm and got off our horses. I was getting better at managing the saddle and thanked Alex for his help.

Dr. B was making his rounds as we were all wrapping up the

day. He approached Alex and me and asked Alex how I was doing. Alex looked at Dr. B and gave him a thumbs-up and a head nod before going back to the farmhouse, before his group got ready to leave.

Dr. B looked at me with a grimace. That's not the face I'd like to see when he was looking at me. But, before I could say anything, he asked me if Alex was talking to me. My double black eyes were what prodded Alex to talk to me, I said.

He retorted, saying how remarkable that was because Alex hadn't spoken with anyone. I told Dr. B that Alex had started the conversation when he asked how I was doing. He then told me how he doesn't like it when people ask him how he got burned. I held my peace, and he eventually said, "It was spontaneous combustion in our farm."

"Wow, Rachel, that's tremendous! I will make a note of how a worker's injury could open the door to conversation", Dr. B said.

I concur, I said, because it was an exciting concept to learn. "Go, Cougars!" I cheered with my post-cheerleading enthusiasm and a big smile. We talked about what had happened, and he asked me to please write a paper about it.

Of course, I agreed. Dr. B then surprised me by asking if I liked football. 'Oh yeah', I answered. He then said he and the football coach are friends and had offered him great tickets for next weekend's game. He then invited me to attend with him! I was so excited, I blurted out, 'Yes!'

Then, I put my foot in my mouth by asking about Tami. "Is Tami your girlfriend!?" I spit out. Dr. B started laughing hard and said, "I'm from Wyoming, and we don't date our cousins or siblings. Tami's my sister! "

Between my black eyes and blushing cheeks, I was sure I looked a colorful mess. Oh, how embarrassing that was. I apologized and held my tongue to prevent any further blunders.

We both laughed, but confirmed the date. A date with Dr. B! That was Christmas come early!

Juicy news!

This deserved a call home, so I picked up my phone and made one. My mom answered and said, "Guess what?" I told her I didn't know. "What?" I asked.

Just then, Jane jumped onto another line and shouted, "Rachel, Vincent asked me to marry him!" She went on to describe how wonderful he was and all the details about him. He was a chemical engineer, a returned missionary who had gone to Taiwan, had five siblings, and loved to hike.

That was a mouthful! I responded by reminding her how tight-lipped she was when we asked about him earlier. I understood now because our brother Jon was a serious electronic engineer and loved his spreadsheets. Jane defended Vincent and said how funny he was.

"One question, Jane," I started. "Does he have a nickname? Like Vin, Vinny?" 'Oh no!' Was her quick response, after which she confirmed that Vincent is a family name. Her Vincent was the fourth Vincent in his family.

"Congratulations, Jane! I'm so happy for you two! I said. There was a lot of discussion amongst the family listening.

Then, I just had to share my news. "Hey guys, I need to share my update. Dr. B asked me to go to the upcoming football game with him, and I have two black eyes!" My family quickly changed the call to FaceTime on speaker.

The chatter escalated with lots of concern and questions. I started by explaining how the Frisbee incident occurred and how it hurt and bled a lot. But seeing me with black eyes had urged my patient to start a conversation, which had never happened. I also explained how Dr. B had asked me to write a paper about it.

My family then couldn't wait for my juicy news about the

football game invite. It happened after the black eye conversation. He told me he was friends with the football coach and that he offered him some good tickets. I confessed to pretty much shouting, "Yes!" when he asked me to the game.

"It's like Christmas came early, and I've never been this excited about anything like this ever!" I squealed. Everyone was happy for me and had me promise to give them all the details after the game.

I love my family and their enthusiasm with me and for me was like a big long-distance hug. These good people were not freaks, and I'll always be grateful for them.

Robin Air still flying

My part-time work with Robin Air continued. My flexible early morning four-hour shifts made that possible, and I enjoyed it. The calls were each different, and I couldn't help using my freak/non-freak litmus testing.

There were enough full- time employees to switch hours with, so I could go home for Christmas. It was a positive workplace with good and varied people. With the amount of activities and competitions, they had made it interesting and enjoyable to be there.

One day alone proved the wide spectrum of calls we received. The woman who called demanding the exact number of cabanas she could reserve was unforgettable. She became irritated and even disgusted when I told her she would need to speak with the resort for that kind of assistance. I confirmed that we were at a call center and unable to access or make reservations for the resorts. That was a head-shaker.

Later, that very same day, I answered a call from a kind gentleman. He needed help canceling an expensive reservation for his family. That normally couldn't be done without a week's notice, I told him. He said that was understandable, but his granddaughter had been murdered, and their family was reeling. So, I went through the proper channels and was able to cancel it for him.

Back to the 27th ward

Going back to church with two of my roommates, Laural and Cathi, the next Sunday was good. The people there were nice and friendly, and the talks in the Sacrament meeting were thought-provoking and evoked a warm feeling.

Sunday school was next, and there were two classes due to the size of our ward. Per usual, a quick verbal roll call was next because we were all getting to know each others' names.

The teacher in our class, Brad, picked on me first. "Did you say your name is Rachel?" he asked pointing at me. I nodded and said 'yes'. He then said he was sure I had a fascinating story behind my double black eyes.

I owed Dr. Smith for his great idea. So, I proceeded to tell the whole group about the microscopic meteor strike that was to blame. NASA is sending their finest experts to examine my nose and the situation, I concluded. There was a mix of head shaking, laughs, and concerned faces.

I then came clean and told them about the errant Frisbee that found my nose. "There's my visual aid on how important honesty is," Brad chuckled.

The class went on well with the jovial group. It was an instructive lesson in many areas. And after the closing prayer, many class members expressed their concern, offered tips on how to get rid of black eyes, and thanked me for sharing my creative black eye story.

The Relief Society President, Veronica, snagged me on my way out and asked me if I could help with the activities committee. I agreed, and she said she'd let me know of our next meeting. I was sure that it would be interesting.

What goes around comes around

The next day, I got a surprisingly good call. Rita had just spoken with her brother, Billy. She said he had just returned from what he calls his 'horse class' and he was so excited to tell her all about it.

I asked her what details he had included and if they had special activities for his horse class. Rita's love for her brother gleamed when she shared what he had done. He said their teacher let them go fast that day, and he was so happy about it. They still had to brush and clean off their horses after the saddles were off.

Billy had told her his horse was like him because he needs to eat and drink. Billy also said the horse needs to get cleaned off, so he's making sure he showers and wears clean clothes. It was great to hear about the enjoyment he was having with equine therapy, AKA, his horse class.

I asked Rita if he had named his horse, and she quickly said, "Sunshine"! She chuckled when she added how Billy knew that name was perfect for his horse.

She surprised me again when she told me my sister, Suzanne, had invited her to a dance. She said they had had a great time and that it would be fun to go again sometime. Having no drinks but water and punch was weird, but that was all right.

Rise and shout!

I couldn't remember being so giddy when I was waiting for Frank, not Dr. B., to pick me up. I wore my most flattering jeans with my farm girl boots and a BYU t-shirt to show my team spirit.

My roommates were in the front room that day. And hearing the knock on the door followed by their giggles let me know Frank had arrived.

Dang, he looked fine! His wavy brown hair was just right. He smelled shower-fresh and was wearing a plaid button-up shirt, Wrangler jeans, and nice cowboy boots. What caught my attention was his big belt buckle that said "Cokeville Champion" on the top and bottom edges.

Wow, that was an ice-breaker right there! I was interested and curious to learn more about this new man in my life. But I need to let the conversation develop naturally. Obviously, I have a habit of asking awkward questions.

My pondering was stopped short when it my roommates stepped forward with big smiles. I quickly introduced Cathi and her friend Judy to Frank. With nods and waves, we made our way out of the apartment.

With his hand on my back, he motioned me towards his truck. It was like when he moved me towards Buttercup on the farm. But, it was just us and he was driving us to the BYU football game!

My eyes weren't as black as they'd been, and Frank noticed that. We chatted without any uncomfortable silences. Then, I told him about Rita's brother Billy and how much he likes his "horse class". He asked me how old Billy was, and I said I didn't know but would ask. Billy had told his sister that his favorite part was when the teacher let him go fast, and we both chuckled.

When I was about to ask him about his belt buckle, he pulled into the VIP parking lot and parked. Just as I was about to open my door, he said, "Stay put." He then hopped out and came around to open my door. I liked this man!

Our seats were excellent, and I commented on how it's good to have connections. "Yep, it is," he replied with a smile. Then I mentioned my curiosity about his belt buckle and congratulated him on the win. He then filled me in on growing up in Cokeville, Wyoming. I asked, "Is that where your interest in equine therapy started?"

He nodded yes and said, "It's a long story, which means we may have to go out again." I couldn't help but smile. The national anthem was then announced. I stood and put my hand over my heart and sang when the music started, and Frank did the same.

The game started, and it was a close one. When the crowd started and stomped their feet on the bleachers, I grabbed Frank's arm. He turned his head to me with a questioning look. I said, "Do you know that sounds exactly like an earthquake and worries me every time?" He asked me if I'd been in an earthquake, and I nodded 'yes' several times.

My attention returned to the game, and I saw a linebacker miss a block. I yelled, "You're not dancing! Take him down!" Frank started busting up laughing. I smiled with my palms up. He didn't realize what a football fan I was.

Frank got up and asked if I'd like to split a chocolate Cougar Tail. "Do ducks quack?" I answered with a smile. He left laughing to go fetch us a Cougar Tail. This was going so well, I thought. Then, I had a flashback of my former failures. Well, I wasn't going to give up on this when it had scarcely started!

The game continued with only a few outbursts on my part. It was so fun. There were a few "Hey, Dr. B!" shout-outs, and he waved. And, so what if I was the teacher's pet?

When the game was over, and we had won, we got up to leave our seats. Frank took my hand naturally as we walked out. I thanked him for inviting me to the game and told him I had a great time.

The drive home was shorter than I wanted it to be. But we had a great time together. He opened my door when we got to my apartment. He took my hand while we walked to the door. Frank then thanked me for the best football game he'd ever been to and kissed the back of my hand.

Juicy news sequel

Calling home in the evening usually caught most people there. Luckily, that was the case this time. Suzanne answered, and I was quick to thank her for befriending Rita. They were developing a good friendship and were planning to go to the next church dance. I congratulated her on the new connection. Then, I told her about talking to Rita about her little brother, who takes a 'horse class' every week.

That got her thinking about what I had called about. "Oh yeah! How's Dr. B?" she shouted. Just then, my mom and Jane were on the call. They had each agreed to change it to a conference call if my call came through. The BYU football game had been the day before, and they knew I was going with him.

"It was perfect!" I started. It was so comfortable talking with him, and we both obviously love the BYU football team. He is aware now that I yell when I'm frustrated at the mistakes the players make. "Armchair Coach" was Dr. B's description of me. And, he said to just call him Frank.

My mom said great and asked if another date would be coming up. I said 'yes' and that he got my door going and coming. I also mentioned that he took my hand going up to the stadium, then back to his truck after the game. Frank said he really enjoyed going to the football game with me.

I knew they would ask. So, I explained how he opened the truck door when we got back to my apartment, held my hand, walked me to the front door, and kissed the back of my hand.

The Petty women gave the date their approval. So, it was a win-win situation because I approved it too.

Back to real life

This first week back after my dream date with Frank, I had to keep my feet on the ground. That wasn't hard because I had homework, class, and work. And, after texting a thank-you note for the wonderful date, I was waiting to hear back from him.

Psychology was the class I was looking forward to because I had done experimenting of my own. It wouldn't be an epiphany to Professor Magleby when I told him about how being so cheerful after my date with Frank attracted positive responses from others. I concluded that dressing up and/or being cheerful is the cure for being more popular.

Professor Magleby then interrupted me by asking if I was talking about Frank Bennion. After I confirmed it, he said, "All right! That's great! I was wondering how long it would take!"

I was surprised and realized they must be friends. "How long after what?" I asked. This was a new twist I wasn't expecting, and I was now very curious. But, before I could say anything, Magleby told me to talk with Frank because it wasn't his place to tell me anymore.

Of course, I couldn't focus on the lecture with that information bait dangling in my mind. I was so curious and didn't know how a conversation about it would play out. I thought of my dad's advice to move forward and let things develop naturally. That would be easier said than done. Or so I thought.

Life is like M&Ms

When you buy a family-size bag of M&Ms, you can't pick the exact color you want without fishing. But, you know they're all delicious. I had been realizing the importance of choosing carefully and trying something new.

When I chose to try Hands-on Equine therapy, it was a happy combination of both. There was no conclusion at first on how this relationship with Frank would develop, but I wanted to give it my best try.

I was tempted to text Frank again, but I needed to focus on my other classes. Spanish 401 was challenging, but it provided me with better vocabulary and grammar.   Elder Hoffman, my blond, blue-eyed Argentine District Leader, set me straight. One day, he let me know that I sounded like a woman selling vegetables in the market! Even our Chilean President, Ayala, told a group of us gringos there was much more Spanish to learn.

Then, Geology was very interesting, and I loved learning the ancient timeline of the Earth's creation. That wasn't the philosophic or social chat room of beliefs. Dr. Smith laid out the periods of the rock formation, including the most well-known era, the Jurassic.

My work at Robin Air filled in most of the gaps in my weekly schedule. However, the missing piece to my puzzle was Frank. I thought he was an intelligent, good, handsome, down-to-earth kind of man, and I was interested.

Team spirit rules!

I had become somewhat comfortable in my limbo until Frank called. It was like a shot of adrenaline. He invited me to BYU's last home football game. Again, I agreed wholeheartedly with a little giggle.

He paused, then said it would be a double date. My history with those made me cringe. However, it would be with his sister and her husband. That sounded safe, but I knew I was being checked out.

My conversation with Professor Magleby had clued me in that something bad had happened in Frank's past. I had no doubt was they were feeling protective of Frank. We hadn't known each other for more than a year, but I wanted the best for him.

My response was genuine when I said, "Well, I've got your back if you have mine." He then thanked me and said he really appreciated that. I continued by saying I really thought highly of him.

We confirmed the date and time for him to pick me up. And, I'm no poker face and told him how excited I was because I had a great time with him at the last game. Frank said he felt the same, then we ended our mutual fan club chat and said goodbye.

Pins and needles

The week and a half before the game felt like a month. I, of course, traded my Robin Air shift for that Saturday quickly because there was no way I was missing that game with Frank.

My Equine therapy class was going to be a little awkward. But seeing Alex's sandy brown hair and blue eyes felt familiar. And his big smile when he saw me made my day. Dr. B (aka my big crush) advised us to prep our horses and follow the trail on the paper he was giving us.

I said 'hi!' to my classmates that were all friends now and waved at Frank. I was all smiles, but that wasn't unusual for me, right?

Alex and I concentrated on our horses and Buttercup was, as usual, easy to work with. Saddling her and getting on that saddle was more successful each week. We were a good team and I loved that he (and Buttercup) trusted me more with each class.

Alex and I stopped our horses side by side and reviewed Dr. B's map. I asked Alex if he wanted to take the lead. He nodded and kicked his horse to get started on our trail. We followed the map perfectly without a word.

"The weather is perfect today," I commented. "Yeah, you like Dr. B don't you?" answered Alex. I was surprised but said, "Yep, I do." The friendship we were developing felt so good.

We finished our ride and headed to the corral. Dr. B trotted up next to us as we unsaddled our horses. He asked if we had any problems following the trail. Alex and I looked at each other and shook our heads no. "But your ears were probably burning," I smiled.

To top the day off, Alex and I started laughing at the same time. Dr. B lowered head towards and looked at us back and forth while raising his hand like a student wanting his teacher's attention. "We'll have to talk, you two," he said with an amused smirk.

An unexpected call

After finishing up on my homework, I started the first world trial of doing laundry. That makes me laugh because it's so straightforward and easy when you have machines doing the work.

In my first area on my mission in Uruguay, we did our laundry in a cement tub with a washboard! I didn't know what I was doing. Our landlady asked me if I wanted a brush, and I refused. I didn't know how I'd use a brush on my clothes.

The funny thing was the brush was almost exactly what I used on Buttercup. My chuckling as I thought about that was interrupted when my phone rang. After hearing Frank's voice after saying 'hello', I was surprised. But, in a good kind of giddy way.

He asked me what I was doing and I embellished the vigorous and complex task of getting my laundry done. Frank laughed with that deep genuine chuckle he had. He then asked what I was doing next and if it was nothing, he'd like to pick me up for a late lunch.

Again, I had those warm trembles he had the effect of producing in me. I said I'd check with my social secretary and get back to him. He paused and didn't say anything. Then I laughed and said I'd love a late lunch with him.

"Great, I'll be there in twenty minutes," Frank said. I agreed, finished the call, and then ran to get dressed. Of course, I checked my hair and makeup. By the time he showed up, I had my favorite green sweatshirt and jeans on.

My roommates shouted asking where I was going. I told them Frank was picking me up for a late lunch. Their cheering stopped cold when the door bell rang.

I opened the door with a big, expectant smile and said, "Hola !" He repeated the greeting and offered me his hand. We walked to his truck and he said the color of my shirt looked great on me.

He opened my door continuing to hold my hand to help me into his truck because it was higher than his car.

He asked me if I had a preferred restaurant. Dolce Vita has good Italian food I responded. He agreed and we headed to that little restaurant in downtown Provo. After parking, he told me to stay put and came around to open my door. Upon entering the restaurant, two or three employees greeted him by name.

So many questions popped through my mind. I was very curious, and we hadn't even been seated yet. My questions could wait until a proper conversation had started.

Your order?

Frank was so likable. Without any awkwardness, he said his favorite there was spaghetti and meatballs. The black-bow tied with white shirt waiter approached the table and nodded at me for my order. I asked for gnocchi and Frank gave him his order.

"How does everyone know your name?" I asked. He said he used to come there a lot and was surprised I wanted that restaurant. "Does it have bad memories for you here?" I asked. My curiosity over rode any tip-toeing and I apologized if it wasn't any of my business.

"No, no" said Frank. "This is a perfect way to fill you in on what was a painful time in my life." He then proceeded to tell me about an old girlfriend that used to like that place. Frank had even proposed and thought everything was great. "But my former best friend was the actual apple of her eye," he frowned shaking his head.

I couldn't help but gasp and shake my head. He concluded with the gritty conclusion that he had actually bought her a wedding ring. The couple ended up eloping and moving to Texas.

"Saya-fetchin-ara" I said. "I hope you were able to sell the ring back." It was a pleasant surprise to realize Frank was doubled over laughing. He said, "I didn't know you could speak Japanese."

Just then, the confused waiter came with our freshly made steaming hot food. We pulled ourselves together and thanked him. After arranging our plates and started eating, the conversation continued.

"I felt so stupid to be in that situation. People were congratulating me and asking where we were registered – dang!" said a sullen Frank. "It was so embarrassing to tell people about the wedding being canceled. Of course, everyone had questions and pressed me for details. It was the worst."

"Frank, dude, she's the stupid one! Any woman that would let a man like you go is the fool" I started. "And, that friend, (I said this with my curled fingers up in the international air quote sign) he's a spineless coward. I don't know details more than what you've just told me, but what you've had to go through really stinks."

"Did you just call me dude, Rachel?" asked Frank. "And what did you mean, a man like me? I'll give you the benefit of the doubt and think it's all positive. Thanks for that, I really appreciate being able to talk with you about this."

"Please take it as the biggest compliment ever, and 'dude' means I really mean what I'm saying don't you know?" I said chuckling. "Frank, you have the best reputation for being tough, qualified and the best social work professor there is. Plus, I've found how nice you are – even to a city girl like me."

This led naturally to a conversation about equine therapy. His first question was if my city girl confessions were true. I covered my eyes and said 'yes'. This led to more laughter, and then I asked him about why he chose to pursue therapy with horses.

He gave me the Reader's Digest version of having friends injured in rodeos. His friend, Tom, got thrown while bull riding and broke his leg. It was a bad break and his horse wanted him close where he could nuzzle up and protect him. So, the horses' behavior is what started his curiosity. And, after seeing the injuries, Frank stuck with barrel racing during rodeos which is where his Cokeville Champion belt buckle was won.

Frank had read the paper I had written about Alex talking to me but had more questions. He knew Alex automatically spoke to me when he had seen my double black eyes. How our conversations continued was really intriguing to him. So he asked me to summarize how the chats increased and if Alex had any anxiety when speaking.

"The only time he withdrew was when I asked him about his skills on the farm," I offered. Frank nodded and said, "Go on" in an encouraging way.

"Well, we had short conversations about how he was burned, if my feet were in the stirrups the right way, which way we should go, and short horse questions," I started. Frank nodded his head and circled his hand with an expectant look in his eyes.

"Are you curious about what we were talking about when I told you your ears must be burning?" I asked. Frank said "yes", so I continued. "This is embarrassing but I mentioned how nice the weather was, Alex paused then said, you like Dr. B don't you? I answered 'yep, I do'".

My cheeks were burning and I was afraid to look up because I didn't know what Frank would say.

"Rachel, that was like Christmas come early," said Frank with a warm smile. "Thanks so much for your honesty – I needed that."

At that point, things changed. He wasn't going to drop to a knee and pop a ring out, but the air felt warm and tingling at the same time.

To offer a sweet off ramp to this late lunch turned dinner conversation, I suggested we top our meal off with some spumoni ice cream.

Missed call

"Hey Rachel, glad you're home!" yelled my roommate Kathy when I came through our apartment's front door. She went on to tell me that she answered my phone when it kept ringing. "You need to call your mom and Jane, and I did confess that Frank had picked you up for a spontaneous lunch date." I answered 'thanks' and told her to hang on when she started throwing out questions about our date.

My head was buzzing and my thoughts were bouncing around like the ball in a pinball machine. It was a positive lunch date, almost too positive. The wrapping paper covering the gift of my relationship with Frank had been torn wide open. Now what? I grabbed my phone off the kitchen counter where I'd forgotten it.

Then I jumped when my sweet mom's call came through, almost dropping the phone. She started by swearing she wasn't spying, but after hearing about my lunch date with Frank she was curious. I gave her the whole low down which took a good twenty minutes and she squealed. I confessed that I loved him and he knew that I, at least, liked him. BYU's last home football game was our next date, but after that there were no plans.

"Well, this is where we come into play," my mom started. "I was sure you were wondering why I had called" she laughed. She explained our one and only Great Aunt Florence wants us to take her to Utah for Thanksgiving. She has cousins there she hasn't seen for years and they contacted her about it."

"So, where do I come into play? I asked. "I'm curious about so many things right now." That's where my mom, the social strategist came into her own. She continued to explain she was trying to have the whole family go to Utah for Thanksgiving. I told her I loved her idea and decided I wouldn't be going home for the holiday, because my family was coming to me!

She gave out a 'woop!' and we talked more about dates and where everyone would stay. I knew at least two of my roommates were going home for Thanksgiving and I'd confirm if Suzanne, Jennifer or Jane could stay in their rooms. She would need to do more planning for our brothers. This would be so fun.

"This will be terrific, and Rachel, I'm so happy for you!!" shouted my mom. "Frank sounds like a great man, and I'm very happy for you both."

"Mom, put the brakes on!" I stated. "We haven't picked out colors, and the wedding cake isn't even in the oven yet." We understood the point I was trying to make, and both laughed.

Girl chat

After talking with my mom, I returned Jane's call to see what was going on and why she had called me. She said she called to catch up, then went right into how she and Vincent were having lots of fun, and even having talks about their future. I told her how fantastic I thought that was.

"Rachel, I'm having the tingles as you would say," she chuckled, then said. "Nothing's set in concrete, but this is going very well. How about you and your cowboy?"

"Oh, Jane, we had a pivotal spontaneous lunch just today, and my mind is still spinning!" I shouted. "Then, Mom just called about all of us having Thanksgiving here in Utah! That's why so many thoughts are going through my mind!"

We both squealed and then took turns filling each other in on details. Neither of us had solid wedding plans. Frank and I hadn't had a talk about our future, but after the lunch we just had, there's no other way it could go. Jane and I wrapped it up, promising to keep each other in touch.

While in the calling mode, I decided to call Laural to thank her for pointing me in the social work direction. It had led me to exactly where I wanted to be. Unfortunately, she didn't answer, and I left a detailed message explaining just those thoughts, hoping she'd call back soon.

Giddy-up

I headed to my Equine Therapy class with butterflies in my stomach. Noticing the van in the parking lot was a relief because I thought I might have thirty or forty minutes to calm down. That was wishful thinking because Frank sprang out of the nearby building and headed right to the driver's seat.

We all greeted him, and he greeted us back and said he'd explain today's lesson on the way to the barn. Soon, he started on how to shoe a horse. I panicked, then saw Maria and Chewy looking confused. I leaned over to them and explained that we would check the horses' hooves to see if they needed to be re-shod. I didn't know how to explain the procedure in English or Spanish, but I'd try.

I could see Frank's face through the rear-view mirror. He saw me and then winked at me with a smile on his face. He said, "Thanks for explaining that to them, Rachel." It was the appreciative professor acknowledging my help, right? I didn't know who else saw that, but I knew I was blushing.

We all chatted on the way to the farm, and I was growing fonder of the rural beauty with each trip out. Dr. B said we were to meet our horses and patients in the barn. Calling him Dr. B instead of Frank was difficult.

The horses were out as well as our patients. I enjoyed this kind of education. Alex and I caught a glimpse of each other right away.

"Hey Alex, my friend!" I shouted with a wave and a smile. He was a little more reserved than usual, and I wondered why. We met up with Buttercup and waited for instructions. I asked Alex if he knew how to shoe a horse, and he nodded yes.

Alex and I gathered our tools and organized our approach. He nodded at me to take the lead, and I immediately started with how-to questions. I threw in a personal question to see how he was doing and if a person asking about his scars was still bothering him.

He lifted one leg back to check on the shoe, then started pulling out the nails. He did that, then replaced a new shoe, hammering in fresh nails. He pointed at me, which was scary and so very new to me. But Alex was experienced and made the steps clear.

"Do you ever wonder why I haven't asked about your scars, Alex?" I asked while pulling back the next leg. This wasn't a guessing game, so I continued. "My dad has scars on forty to fifty percent of his body, so I'm very aware of how burns damage the body."

I had his attention, and he asked if that was true. He then expertly corrected my nailing as we chatted and took care of Buttercup's remaining hooves. I confirmed that my dad has lots of scarring that we don't even notice now. I told him how hard it was when I was little to have people stare at his scars when we were at the swimming pool or the water park.

"It made me feel very protective of him and how I feel now about you, Alex," I stated as we were now standing face to face. "My dad was playing in his backyard when some stupid kids in the field behind his house lit matches, and you know how fast dry grass catches fire and spreads."

Alex dropped his head and nodded, then said quietly, "I sure do." I noticed that he was crying and gave him a big hug. I'm sure that wasn't the professional thing to do, but we're humans who need support and caring.

"How's it going over here, you two? Buttercup looks great!" said Dr. B as he came around checking on everyone.

"Well, as you know, this city girl could not have done it without Alex," I said with a smile as we backed up.

"Alex, I could tell you stories about what a city girl Rachel is," laughed Dr. B. "She didn't know potatoes grew underground!"

What happened next was classic when Alex threw back his head laughing and asked, "Is that true?" I answered, "Yes, it is," with a smile and palms up as if confessing.

"Hey Frank, you could read my list of city girl confessions to give everyone something to laugh about," I chuckled.

"You should!" Alex shouted. "I'd like to hear it."

We were very surprised to hear him talk, and Dr. B (Frank) turned to me with a tilted head and questioning look. I smiled and gave him a thumbs-up. He went to his office to get my original paper.

"Hey guys, before Dr. B gets out here to announce today's agenda surprise, I need to have my own back and give you a little of my background," I started. "I'm from San Fernando, California which is at most 600 feet above sea level. I've never had a white Christmas and our family garden had above ground vegetables, except the carrots, of course. And, we went to the beach not the mountains. So, what you'll hear is true!"

The party that followed was an organic (as in authentic), friend-created and humorous good time.

Game day!

Kathy and Julie chose to do their homework in the front room while I finished getting ready for Frank to pick me up for the BYU football game. I went downstairs and asked if I looked all right. My roommates gave me a unanimous 'YES!' The doorbell rang, and after racing to answer the door, they started cracking up and swung the door open.

"No way!" I shouted. "We're wearing the same sweatshirt!" Frank came in laughing at our matching royal blue sweatshirts with a big block 'Y' on the front.

"You two look like a match made in heaven!" laughed Kathy.

"Should I change my shirt?" I asked feeling a bit embarrassed. But Frank smoothed things over like I'd learned he had the skill to do. He was good at making people feel comfortable.

"Please leave it on! You look great, and that makes me look a little better," Frank chuckled. "Plus, my sister Tami and her husband Brad will be sitting with us, so we should get going to meet them there."

I mouthed 'Wish me luck!' to my roommates who were all smiles as we walked out of the apartment.

After Frank walked me out to his car, he opened the passenger-side door and made sure I was seated before closing the door. He got seated and immediately asked, "Rachel, how did you get Alex talking? What broke the ice?"

"Well Frank, you don't know this about me, but my father has scars on almost half of his body from being burned when he was a kid. I told Alex about it and how protective I felt when people stared at his scars," I began. "Stupid kids playing with matches in the knee-high grass behind his house started the fire. My dad was surrounded by the fire and he climbed up the jungle gym in their backyard to get away. Luckily, his next-door neighbor saw what was going on, reached through the flames, and pulled him out. I told Alex that's why I understand his anxiety when people look at him, and why I feel protective about him."

"Oh my, Rachel, you're right, I didn't know that about you!" shouted Frank. "Is that when you hugged?"

"Yes, but I hugged him because he was tearing up and it was the natural, caring thing to do," I finished.

We pulled into the stadium parking lot and walked up to the stadium hand in hand. Frank squeezed my hand and whispered, "I'm so impressed with you."

Kick-off time

We found our seats, and Frank led the way, so he was on my right-hand side. So, when Tami and Brad arrived, we stood up to greet them. When all of the introductions and handshakes were over, we got seated.

"Do you guys always dress alike?" asked a laughing Brad.

"No, we don't, but Rachel has good style like me!" smiled Frank. "So, it worked perfectly."

"Frank, you're a cowboy, you're not concerned with fashion. And Rachel, I'm so glad to meet you!" chirped Tami, flashing bright blue eyes fringed by her straight blonde hair. "Frank doesn't get out much these days, so I'm pleasantly surprised to have you here."

"Well, lucky me then. I love these football games and Dr. B, AKA Frank, is a great guy!" I said, trying to be as perky as Tami. My brown eyes and auburn hair were an attractive combination, if I do say so myself.

"Tami, Rachel's a sideline coach like you! So, this will be fun," Frank said.

Tami and I looked at each other and smiled. She and I were sandwiched between Brad and Frank.

"Rachel is my favorite student because she's brilliant and chose my class!" Frank continued.

I was blushing, because after our last lunch and the information we shared, we were shaking down where our relationship was going.

Back to the game, we paid close attention to how the Cougars were doing.

As one of the linebackers missed his tackle, I shouted, "Have you ever heard of a shoestring tackle 23? Anything, just take him down!" Tami and I gave each other five and nodded. The team played a little better for the next quarter.

When the crowd started stomping their feet, I held onto Frank's arm, and Tami looked over to see what I was doing.

"That sounds just like an earthquake and gives me the chills," I said. "I'm from California and have had my share of earthquakes."

"It's a perfect time to be sitting next to her so she can grab my arm," Frank said. "Hey, who wants a Cougar tail? Split one Rachel?" I nodded, and he and Brad left to buy the treats.

"Hey, Rachel, we were wondering about your plans for Thanksgiving," began Tami. "Were you planning on going home?"

That question started a big conversation when I told her my mom had just called the day before about this. My parents were coming to Utah with my Great Aunt Florence and as much of our family as possible. I told her I was checking with my roommates and asked if my sisters could use their rooms if they came up. We started nodding as the Thanksgiving plans were coming together.

"I'll give my family the dates so they'll have time to book some hotel rooms," I stated, and was totally surprised by Tami's response.

"No! Your family can stay at the farmhouse, and that's where we can eat!" she exclaimed. "If you and Frank are hitting it off, which it seems like you are, eating together would be a great idea!"

Frank and Brad returned with the Cougar tails and drinks, and we filled them in on our Thanksgiving discussion.

"That's great!" said Frank with a grin.

We got eating and paying attention to the game. I caught Frank's eye and gave him a questioning look with my palm up. He nodded several times and smiled.

Just then, the quarterback threw a long pass, and we held our breath. The catch was made, and we cheered. The next play started with the offense scrambling a bit.

"Come on, O line!! Protect your quarterback!" yelled Tami, and we smiled and bumped knuckles. She's a lot of fun, I thought. The Cougars scored.

We had a very nice time, and I was able to ask Tami and Brad about their jobs and pursuits. These were people I wanted to get to know more.

Now, BYU was playing defense, and the opposing team was good. We yelled and clapped as the game moved on. One of the BYU players was having a hard time tackling,

"You're not dancing! Knock him down!" I shouted. Frank and I gave each other five.

The game was a great battle, and BYU won. We turned to leave the stadium and headed to the parking lot where we hugged and promised to keep in touch.

On our way home, Frank and I talked without pause. The interests we shared greased the wheels of our conversation.

"Rachel, if you're worrying about Thanksgiving, don't," stated Frank bluntly. "We like each other, right? And it would be fantastic to meet each other's parents." I nodded in agreement with my mind reeling.

When we got to my apartment, Frank opened my door and helped me out. He stood still and looked at me.

"Before we're interrupted, I would love a hug and a kiss," Frank said with a big smile. I loved his 'no games' approach; he was so handsome and smart, and he smelled good- just out of the shower good.

So, his arms wrapped around me and we kissed. It was a slow, soft, long kiss, and I was in heaven. We looked at each other again sincerely.

"Hmm, Frank, I could do that forever!" I said quietly with a smile.

"Rachel, I love your honesty, and I love you!" he sweetly said.

What a lovely blur

Wow, I was so happy! My classes, tests, and work were jumbled together. Yet, even with so much going on in my mind, I was focused and driven to have things go well. With Thanksgiving just a few days away, and finals right around the corner, I was a little tense.

Psychology was the first class I had after the best football game ever. It was the perfect class to start with because Professor Magleby was the first person I saw, and he saw me. He walked closer and quietly said, "Matching sweatshirts"?

"We didn't plan on it! You must have been there." I stated not wanting to start any conversation with the classroom filling up. He persisted and asked if everything was going well with a big smile on his face. I nodded yes with a smile of my own. Like I've said, I'm no poker face.

"I'm so happy for you two, Rachel. I think you're exactly what Frank needed." Professor Magleby gushed.

I patted him on the arm with a reminder that nothing was set in stone yet. But I appreciated his support. How Frank and Professor Magleby became friends was something I planned on getting some answers to.

After that class, I walked to the science building for my Geology class. Classmate friendships had firmed up as the semester moved along. They were a great group of people.

That night, I worked a remote shift for Robin Air, which was pretty slow. It gave me time to wonder and ponder about details. I about fell out of my office chair when the doorbell rang. My roommates yelled about opening the door, and I had five more minutes until my shift was finished. So, I stayed put.

"How's my favorite Robin Air employee?" Frank shouted as

he came into my bedroom/office. He had big milkshakes from the Cougareat. I smiled and paused my calls until another minute had passed. I removed my headset, and after signing off from the computer, I told Frank there were rules about men coming into women's bedrooms.

Frank chuckled as he headed into the kitchen to set the shakes down on the table.   I introduced him to my roommates, who were trying to move around the kitchen nonchalantly. He was a real gentleman and made them each feel noticed and complimented in various ways.

"You've gained some fans," I said as my roommates scattered away to give us some privacy. "But, please know that I'm President of your fan club and would love a smooch." I smiled, then leaned over to kiss Frank.

"You're pretty forward, little lady," Frank smiled. "With me, I like that."

Our milkshakes, mint chocolate for me and his peanut butter chocolate, tasted better than ever. We chatted about the football game, and he mentioned how much Tami and Brad liked me. That led to Thanksgiving and the fact that my parents, four siblings, and Great Aunt Florence were coming. Yikes! I asked Frank if that would really be okay.

"Two of my sisters will be staying here in my apartment. Some of my roommates are going home for Thanksgiving and are fine with sharing their rooms," I explained. "My brothers, Jon and Will, must be feeling protective about their little sister to make this trip."

We continued to hold hands and chat until the clock surprised us with how late it was. We stood up for a quick goodbye hug and a kiss. Frank confirmed with me that I would be in his class the next day. And, I told him there was no other place I'd rather be.

And, the next day, I was there and experienced a great lesson.

Dr. B asked us students to let our patients take the lead and choose what we should do. For me, it was heartening to see how empowered Alex felt to be the one in charge. That was an important milestone to see.

I had helped, but didn't do much more than be a friend to him. When we met, he would hardly speak or make eye contact.   But now he took control, made sure my saddle was secure, and that I was ready to go. And like Rita's little brother, Billy, Alex chose to have us trot. He knew my lack of cowgirl experience, so we didn't go fast but had a great time. And, I got a wink, smile, and thumbs up from Frank.

Turkey day at the Bennion farm!

The day before Thanksgiving was so much fun. I loved seeing and hugging everyone. Everyone except Jane had come because she needed to stay with her Vincent. My family arrived separately, and we all met at Chuck-A-Rama for dinner, which was Great Aunt Florence's idea. She grew up in Utah, and it had been her favorite.

On our way to the Bennion farm the next day, they all grilled me about Frank and my equine therapy. I gushed about him, the class, and our amazing BYU football games. I also mentioned him calling me Ginger due to my hair color, and they laughed.

My mom asked me if I loved Frank, and I admitted that I did. That caught everyone's attention and encouraged more questions. They asked if we had kissed and if he had asked me to marry him. I answered yes to the kissing and no to the proposal.

Our conversation stopped when we arrived at the Bennion farm. Suddenly, Tami burst out from the front door with a big smile and a wave. She encouraged us to come into the house. I grabbed the chocolate pie I had made, and we all jumped out and headed in.

"Hey, Rachel! Is that Frank?!" shouted Aunt Florence as she pointed to him with her snow white curls bouncing. I nodded and smiled over to Frank. "Wow, he's a real looker! That's a prime cut kind of man with a cute little bahoochie!"

"Aunt Florence!" shouted an embarrassed Jennifer.

Frank covered his eyes while he laughed. I was blushing and embarrassed, but I introduced myself and my family to the Bennions I knew. When Frank's mom and dad realized I didn't know their names, they took over with the introductions. George was their other son, and he was there with his wife Lucy and their two little kids. Tami and Brad nodded at me and said 'nice to meet you' with a wave to the Petty family in general.

"Who's the livestock grader I heard scoring my grandson?" called an elderly man walking into the room. We all pointed at our Great Aunt Florence, and he candidly checked her out.

"Everyone, this is my grandpa, Orson Bennion!" said Frank. I hadn't met him, and we all waved and smiled at him.

"That was me, mister!" said Great Aunt Florence with a pointed look at Grandpa Bennion. "And, I'd say you look like a juicy pork chop." Everyone was laughing at their geriatric flirting.

"Hey, order up, everyone!" shouted Frank's dad, Samuel. "So, please hush up, you two, and come to the table. Hey Bill, would you please offer a blessing on this feast?" My dad stood up to pray and did so. My mom had already been making herself useful in the kitchen with Samuel's wife, Sharon.

Frank and I sat next to each other. Orson did make a point to sit next to Florence, and they started chatting right away. She noticed his stone bolo tie and asked him if he was a rockhound. He nodded yes and asked her if she had ever gone to Delta, Mineral Fork, or Dugway because there was good digging there. She said she'd only been to Delta but would like to try those others he'd mentioned, and their conversation continued.

We all chatted to get to know each other better. It reminded me of going to a singles' ward because I knew the Bennions were checking us out, and me especially, as a potential member of their family. And we were reviewing them as well. It was all good, and there was a real amiable feeling between us.

"Rachel, Frank says you're becoming a great cowgirl social worker," said Samuel. I looked at Frank with a questioning look and said, "I'm sure trying, but have so much still to learn."

"I told my family here all about how Rachel's compassion and patience have helped one young man to talk and make eye contact," boasted Frank. "This kid hadn't been opening up to anyone.

However, I think her double black eyes really broke the ice."

All surprised eyes turned to me, and I laughed and nodded in agreement. Then, I told them about the Frisbee incident and how I took my geology teacher's explanation that it must have been a microscopic meteor hit. I then whined about how the NASA experts never showed up to research the episode with a big smile, and then everybody laughed.

"Rachel, you need to tell us more! I'm sure you haven't even told us everything that went on during your mission," said Suzanne.

This created a flurry of mission questions about my mission and new inquiries about the others' missions.

"Well, Suzanne, there are some things you don't want to worry your moms about, and I'm sure you other return missionaries here have great tales to tell," I started, which caught my parents and Frank's attention.

"My mission was pretty straightforward. I learned Spanish well, and the people in Uruguay are wonderful, so it was a pleasure to teach and provide service to them. I caught a few colds, avoided tarantulas and snakes, endured the humidity, sprained my ankle, which stunk because we didn't have a car or bicycle, but the most dangerous thing was the men always gathering around us and offering to buy us a drink. I was never really scared, except one day, one of the men grabbed my arm. I just yanked my arm out of his grasp, and we kept walking. And that's enough about me."

There were some appreciative nods, gasps, and smiles. And, we all continued to chat and eat the delicious food. It was so enjoyable to speak and get to know the Bennion family. All of us really enjoyed getting to know each other, and any Freak Magnet litmus test was becoming a stupid memory. These were good people, and judging them or anyone with a general thumbs up or thumbs down would be so shallow and so wrong.

"Sharon, this is all so delicious, and thanks to you and Samuel for your hospitality!" I said. Everyone agreed and had really enjoyed each others' company. Everybody started standing as we were getting ready to leave. That's when Grandpa Orson spoke up, saying, "Are there any announcements to be made?"

This was so embarrassing, and Frank and my dad were nowhere to be seen. There was an awkward stir until Tami broke the silence.

"Hey Grandpa, as it stands, no one has any announcements," she said with a big smile. "But stay tuned because there may be some updates coming up!"

"Well, me and my little sugar snap Flo here and I want to catch a ride to one of our many rock pits around here," smiled Grandpa Bennion. "Any volunteers to be our tour guide?"

I was surprised when my brothers stepped up, saying they'd like to see more of Utah and would take them. At about this time, my dad and Frank had quietly merged back into the crowd. My dad put his arm around me and kissed my head. I looked up and saw his warm smile and little nod. I felt his warmth and approval of whatever conversation he'd had with Frank.

Details were being made with the rock hunters as we all hugged each other. Again, these Bennions were good people, and I was getting excited about the possibility of joining the group. As a master of good timing, Frank appeared next to me. He hugged and kissed me as the surrounding family watched and smiled in appreciation.

There was a good feeling as we said our goodbyes. My mind was spinning at the thought that my life was about to change.

"Rachel, honey, I have some cowboying to do this weekend, but I'll see you in class on Monday," said Frank.

"Sounds like a plan, Frank," I said with a big smile.

This felt like a good Monday

Thanksgiving was indeed a cornucopia of everything good. On Saturday, we had a Petty women's trip to the mall. And, of course, we found some real victory purchases. Church yesterday was strengthening to my faith and testimony of Jesus Christ and His gospel. And I was ready to kick off my week with my favorite class.

Little did I know what was to come. I was wearing the cute pink cashmere sweater and great-smelling perfume I bought on Saturday. And in the van going to the farm, we all chatted about our Thanksgivings and the basic topics of the day. When we pulled into the farmhouse driveway, there was a big sign on the fence. It said, 'Come right into the farmhouse den' and there were arrows pointing the way.

I saw Garth already there with a big smile. And the rest of us filed in and picked a seat. Chewy then asked me to switch places with Maria so they could sit together. We made the change, and it left me front and center. Garth moved to the back row with his camera, saying Dr. B asked him to record the class for the Equine Therapy library. This was unusual but feasible, so we all sat still. There were more back-and-forth smiles, and it felt like something was going on.

That's when Dr. B (my Frank) came in, offering to say the opening prayer. That was abrupt, but it's when I noticed our patients joining the group that I could see something was going on. This was unusual and surprising when Frank began to pray.

"Dear Heavenly Father, we're grateful to be together and pray that Thou will be present. And, I pray for Thy Spirit to be with Rachel Petty when I ask her to marry me so she will say 'Yes' in the name of Jesus Christ, amen."

He kneeled before me and presented a diamond ring and said,

"Rachel, you're the best thing that's happened to me, and I love you. Will you marry me?"

I was stunned as we looked each other in the eyes. This was really happening!!

"Frank, I love you too, and it would be a privilege to be your wife," I cried with a big smile as he placed the ring on my finger and we hugged and kissed. The whole group laughed, cried, and smiled with us. Alex caught my eye with a grin and thumbs up.

There was happy commotion, and Frank held my hand while we answered questions. When will your marriage date be? What'll be your colors? Which temple will you be sealed in?

"Guys, you can see this just happened, and we haven't decided on those details," I interrupted. "But, we will keep you all informed."

"This has been so fun, and thanks for recording it for our families, Garth," said Frank. "This class has been the best, and I'm glad we could share this spontaneous proposal with you. But know your final essay I outlined will still be due on Friday. And, there are cookies and soda to celebrate this in the barn."

Final essay per Professor Frank

Rachel Petty

Hands-On Equine Therapy

I've learned so much in your class. Horses used to intimidate me, but I learned how to coexist with them, shoe them, groom them, feed them, and make sure they had plenty of water. It became a friendship which I really came to enjoy. And, it has felt like an accomplishment.

I need to get more book-smart about sociology and psychology, but it's going well, and I enjoy it. It's fascinating to learn about people. I feel the more I connect with others, the better I know how to help them.

Having a "patient" was also new and intimidating, but Alex will always be my friend now. Dr. B's advice to match the speed of the horses and patients was important. Alex knows so much more about horses than I, but he was patient, and we came to appreciate each other. He was genuinely concerned when he saw me with two black eyes, and that opened up our communication. He told me he didn't like it when people stared at him and asked him about his scars.

That was a stroke of serendipity because my dad has about fifty percent of his body covered with scars due to a burning accident when he was a kid. When I told Alex that, he was surprised, but I confirmed it really happened. Then I told him I didn't like it when people stared at his stared at his scars. It made me feel protective, and that's how I feel about Alex. When I told him that, he started weeping, and I gave him a big hug.

I didn't know if that was something professional social workers do. But it felt like the human and caring thing to do. After he saw my flaws and knew that I had his back, we were a team.

Will I continue with Equine Therapy? If Dr. B's still teaching it, oh yes. And, we plan to live happily ever after!

My freak magnet conclusion

The chiasmic ending of this book will explain how I was labeled a Freak Magnet, but now reject that label. No one can be deeply accurate when judging others. Everybody came from somewhere and has had personal experiences we'll never know.

For example, I'll never know the back story of that frail little woman asking me for money on my mission. But, I like to think she had loving parents and was their most precious little daughter when she was a cute baby, toddler, and little girl. Who knows what difficulties came her way? And who or what had failed her.

And that dingy-looking man who walked right up to us on the road and spoke perfect English was intriguing. My first guess is that he was an expatriate from the United States who chose to live in Uruguay. He seemed happy and may have had a wife, children, and a job. It will never be known, but hopefully, he enjoyed a good life in Uruguay.

One back story that I sadly do know is that of my friend Trina (not her real name). We were friends, went to church together, and played on the high school's softball team. It turned out her dad beat her and was physically abusive to the whole family.

In the Los Angeles area, there were lots of bars where she could stay as late as possible. She did this to stay away from her house. Then she started taking Speed (AKA Methamphetamine) so she could stay awake during class the next day. It was impossible to know exactly what was happening at the time. I learned more of these details after graduation.

But when Trina called, and we talked the day after I returned from my mission, it was a brief conversation. I was settled into my beliefs and happiness, and I wasn't going to move in with her and her girlfriend near the beach. I hope she's doing well.

And as a former Freak Magnet, I now refuse to label people. I suggest getting to know someone and giving them the benefit of the doubt. It took me years, travel and experiences to calm my critical mind and enjoy the many good people there are in the world.

9 7 9 8 9 0 3 2 1 0 7 8 7